The Secret Friend

The Secret Friend

Our Journey

By Susan Bostian

Copyright

Cover Image

The Journey

Above the mountains
the geese turn into
the light again

Painting their
black silhouettes
on an open sky.

Sometimes everything
has to be
inscribed across
the heavens

so you can find
the one line
already written
inside you.

Sometimes it takes
a great sky
to find that

first, bright
and indescribable
wedge of freedom
in your own heart.

Sometimes with
the bones of the black
sticks left when the fire
has gone out

someone has written
something new
in the ashes
of your life.

You are not leaving.
Even as the light fades
quickly now,
you are arriving.

David Whyte, [The Journey], from [The House of Belonging]. ©
[2022] DavidWhyte. Reprinted with permission from David
Whyte and Many Rivers Company, LLC, Langley, WA
www.davidwhyte.com.

Table of Contents

Acknowledgments

My thanks and love go out to Abbey for being my friend, teacher, and co-adventurer for a life-changing year. My thanks and love also to John for inviting me to walk with him for part of his challenging journey.

I would like to thank my loving daughter, Catherine, for all her help and support throughout this project. I would also like to thank my wonderful son, Jason for his entrepreneurial inspiration. My two children are an immeasurable source of love and joy.

I would also like to thank my entire family for a lifetime of love, friendship, and unfaltering belief in me. Special thanks to my sister, Nancy, who brought her wits and wisdom to California to be a second Secret Friend to Abbey. Another special thanks to my sister, Maddie (Jeannie) for her encouragement and bonding over our shared love of steamed clams!

I would also like to acknowledge all caregivers everywhere who give themselves with love, to make life better for others.

Also, to all my special friends and Zumba dancers—keep showing up! Stay wild and dance with joy!

Dedication

This book is dedicated to my three magical grandchildren,

Christian, Jacqueline, and Everett! You inspire me to dance like no one is watching, follow my dreams, and keep my promises!

Thank you, dear Christian, Jacqueline, and Everett. I love you more than you could ever imagine, and I will keep working to make you proud.

Chapter 1 December
The Season of Darkness and Tears

She's Not All There

For one year, I was paid to be a Secret Friend. And, for one year, my friend and I laughed and cried, charmed the Cheshire Cat, danced with a Voodoo Priestess, chased peacocks, fought off pot-bellied pigs, broke some rules, seized every moment, and created a world where imagination and reality collided.

We became the best of friends, even though our friendship was based on a lie. Each day I would slip into my role, convince her we were going to a happy place, and we would head out into the world in search of a magical adventure.

I wanted to find the miracle that would fix both of us. In the beginning, I thought we were trying to outrun a devastating diagnosis and a disastrous divorce. In the end, we stumbled and fell into a wonderland where everything and nothing made sense.

I was hired by her husband to accompany her out into the world and provide her with a sense of normalcy. She was losing her mind. Early-Onset Alzheimer's was stealing her memory, her identity, and her independence.

She was only sixty-two years old, but sometimes she forgot her address, her phone number, and the way back home. I was recovering from a terrible divorce. Someone had stolen my address, my phone number, and my husband. There was no way back home.

It all began with an innocent greeting. I left my apartment building to go for my morning walk. We live in beautiful Palo Alto, California, on the edge of a creek that rises and falls dramatically with the seasons.

In winter, the waters come crashing down the narrow ravine threatening to overflow the banks and wreak havoc. By summer, the water has disappeared, exposing a rocky bottom littered with broken tree limbs that have fallen during the harsh winter storms. On this December morning, I could hear the water roaring and I noticed the bare roots of a newly toppled tree.

As I walked over to assess the damage, I recognized a tall man walking toward me as he left the apartment building next to mine. He was handsome in that East Coast, stiff jaw, rimless glasses, and proper manners kind of way. I had noticed him in our communal swimming pool and admired his attentive, caring concern toward his wife.

"Why hadn't I married someone like that?" I remembered thinking at the time. She was pretty and athletic looking. They looked like the perfect couple.

I smiled and said, "Good Morning. How are you?"

He stopped in the middle of the road. "How am I?" Suddenly he burst into tears. "I'm terrible. I can't take it anymore."

The Secret Friend

Details of fights, sleep deprivation, and phone calls from the police, came bursting out. "My wife has Alzheimer's, and she wants me to just stay home with her. But I can't. I have to go to work."

Startled, I grasped for words. "Actually, I met her once in the laundry room. She had mixed everyone's clothes together and she didn't know which ones were hers. I thought something might be wrong."

"You should see our apartment," he said, "Dishes are on the floor, clothes are on the table, there's food in the bathroom. Today she wanted to wear two different shoes. I tried to get her to change them. She got mad and threw me out of the apartment."

"You know, I've also seen her riding her bike downtown in the middle of the street." I had wanted to tell someone ever since I had watched her wobbling dangerously close to the oncoming traffic.

"She grew up around here. The streets are imprinted on her brain." He wiped away the tears and shrugged his shoulders.

"But she might get hit by a car."

"Well, if that happens, at least she will go doing something she loved."

"What?"

"Look, this is a new reality for me. I can't even play tennis or go sailing without feeling guilty."

"What does she do all day?"

"She sits in the apartment and listens to the radio, or she looks at old photographs. Sometimes she goes out and gets lost."

"Does she have an identification bracelet?" My maternal instinct had kicked in.

"No. She won't admit there's anything wrong with her."

"What happens when she gets lost?"

"It depends. She has a note in her purse, but a lot of the time she loses her purse."

"So how does she get home?"

Sometimes, someone finds her and either they help her get home, or they call me from her cell phone, and I have to go get her."

At this point all the stranger danger scenarios are playing in my head. "Maybe you could hire someone to help her."

"No. She refuses to accept a caregiver. I took her to the adult day care center and I even told her that she was a volunteer not a patient, but she figured it out. She ran out the door screaming, and she won't go back."

"So, what are you going to do?"

He started crying again. "I only have one idea left before I put her in some kind of nursing home."

"What's your idea?"

The Secret Friend

"I need to find a Secret Friend for her. Someone who would take her out for a walk or coffee and act like her friend. I would pay for them without her knowing. She just wants to feel normal."

I considered the implications of this unusual proposal. Then, I noticed he was staring intently at me.

"This might be presumptuous, but would you be interested in taking her out?"

The challenge sounded intriguing. The deception made me feel uncomfortable. But the truth is, I was drowning financially.

"How often would you want someone?"

"Maybe two days a week, for a few hours each day. Just to get her out of the apartment."

"Actually, I just went through a divorce. I need to get a full-time job, but I could probably help out for a while."

"Really? That would be great. Maybe we could go out for coffee and discuss it."

I felt awkward. "Maybe."

He had brightened considerably. "Hey, I have a sailboat. Maybe we can go sailing sometime."

"Maybe." I was feeling weird about this whole idea.

"By the way, my name is John. Wait, I have a business card. Call me or send me an email. Let's talk about this some more."

"Hi, I'm Susan."

He smiled appreciatively. "I want to pay you for this. Ten dollars an hour seems too little, but I think twenty seems like too much."

I smiled tentatively. "Around here, even the babysitters get twenty dollars an hour."

Suddenly, he leaned over and gave me a big hug. "Thank you so much."

"I'm glad I can help."

He got into a big, blue BMW and drove away.

I immediately called my sister to get her advice. "Nancy, what do you think about this?"

"You need a job, and he needs a caregiver for his wife. Take it. Is he cute?"

"Nancy! He's married."

"Yeah, but she has Alzheimer's, and it sounds like she's not all there."

This is how I tumbled down a rabbit hole into the foggy world of moral and ethical landmines, uncomfortable suggestions, and unthinkable dilemmas, otherwise known as Alzheimer's.

CHAPTER 2 JANUARY

The Starbucks Solution

John and I exchange several rounds of emails. He suggests a few scenarios where we would all accidentally run into each other. The options sound too rehearsed and obvious. He sounds skeptical about my chances of convincing her to leave the apartment without him. The holidays intervene and life rushes by. It's January by the time we finally agree that I will go over and talk to her on my own.

I'm feeling nervous as I ring her downstairs buzzer. I have been considering several alternative stories about why I am showing up and asking her if she wants to go somewhere. She buzzes me upstairs without asking who is at the door. As I get off the elevator, I see her standing in the hallway looking around.

I am not sure if she recognizes me. I decide to keep it simple. "Hi. How are you?"

She smiles. "Good. Whatcha doing?"

"I'm going to Starbucks for coffee, and I wondered if you wanted to go with me."

"Sure. Let me get my purse." There is no hesitation. She wants to go.

I follow her into her apartment. The devastation is evident. Piles of photographs are strewn across the living room floor. Books, magazines, and clothes cover every possible surface. A bag

7

of potting soil is ripped open, and she appears to be re-potting several plants on the heavily stained, once-white carpet. The sliding glass doors to the balcony are wide open. I need to say something.

"I like your place. It's so bright and sunny."

"Yeah. All this stuff is mine. I have more stuff, but I don't know where it is."

The living room has only one chair and a sofa. A huge, flat screen television is propped against the wall and the weatherman is rambling on about the chance of rain. The furniture does not match my expectations. The decor is early college days, sparse, temporary, not built to last.

"Your dining room table is beautiful." The round, pedestal table appears to be solid oak and fills the adjacent dining room. It is also covered with papers, unopened mail, jewelry, and coffee mugs.

"My family gave me that. They gave me a lot of nice things, but I don't know what happened to them. I think my husband is stealing things from me."

I'm not sure how to answer this, but I think we should stick to happy subjects. I walk out onto the balcony.

"You have a great garden out here."

The balcony is crowded with brightly colored ceramic pots filled with a variety of plants. Most are barely clinging to life. She points to a withered geranium with a faded red flower dangling on the end of a dehydrated branch.

"That's from my father's funeral. It's really special to me."

"Oh, I'm sorry. Did he die recently?"

"Yeah. He had Alzheimer's. Ok. I'm ready to go."

I notice her cell phone and house keys on the dining room table.

"Do you want to bring your phone and keys?"

She places her pocketbook down on a chair and walks over to the table to retrieve the keys and phone.

"Ok," she says, laughing, "Now I'm ready to go."

"Me, too. I really need some coffee today."

I discretely pick up her purse and head for the door. She walks out making no effort to close the door. I hold her purse on my arm so she will notice.

"Hey! How did you get my purse?" She asks, more amused than upset.

I pretend to be surprised. "I'm always picking things up. I guess it's from being a mommy."

We laugh together at how silly I am. I hand her the purse, and we are off.

The Field of Dreams

"Have you ever seen the creek?" she asks me excitedly as we leave the building. As I nod, she tells me she played in the creek when she was a little girl.

"We used to pick blackberries along the creek." she says, "C'mon, I'll show you." She is thrilled to be my tour guide. Her degree is in botany, and she is pointing out different plants and trees as we hike along the rushing water. "These eucalyptus trees aren't native, but I like the way they smell," she says confidently.

"What's this bush?" I ask, enjoying our little game.

"Don't touch that plant. It will make you itch," she instructs me. "I want my own garden, so I can grow flowers."

"You can grow plants on your balcony."

"I don't like living in an apartment. I want a house, a garden, and a dog. I told John if he doesn't get those things for me, I'm going to get a divorce."

I wonder if my dreams are as unlikely to come true as hers.

She seems happy walking and talking, and I am happy to follow her lead. We can easily walk into town, it's only about three miles round trip. I wonder if she has any idea who I am.

She tells me her parents met in college and she is a native Californian. Her father was a builder, who built a school just for her.

The Secret Friend

She worked for a newspaper. I tell her I was associate editor at a newspaper back east.

"Do you work?" she wants to know. I need a good reason to explain why I am not working now.

"I'm a writer, but it's hard for me to concentrate during the day. So, I like to do things during the day and write at night."

"I want to get a job. Maybe working with animals or plants. I worked at Alcatraz."

"When we first moved here, my kids wanted to go to Alcatraz, but I thought it might be too scary," I say, "but, sometimes I wish I had taken them and left them overnight." She laughs and I am impressed that she gets my joke.

"I can't get a job because I can't drive. I hit some woman, but it wasn't a big deal," she shakes her head.

"What happened?"

"I was driving to the bookstore, and they were standing in the road. It wasn't bad. They really didn't need to call the police."

"Did anyone get hurt?"

She seems unsure. "I don't think so. But they called my husband and he won't let me drive anymore. I'm really mad about it. I still want to drive."

"I know what you mean. I love to drive. In fact, you're welcome to come with me, whenever you want."

"Thanks. Hey, my name is Abigail, but you can call me Abbey."

"I'm Susan."

"Good. Did we get coffee yet?"

Stealing Subaru's

As we approach an intersection downtown, Abbey notices a car pulling into the street.

"That's my car" she says as she walks into the road without looking for oncoming traffic. I am conditioned by years of walking with children to be at her side immediately. Luckily, there are no other vehicles in sight. The woman driving the car in question rolls down her window.

"What did you say?" she asks as Abbey walks toward her car.

"Is this my car? My husband keeps letting his friends use my car."

I'm half a step behind Abbey and I give the driver a sign to disregard us and drive on. The woman quickly understands my gesture. "No, this is my car. Have a nice day." She smiles and drives away.

I realize that I have a skill set from raising children and many of these tools are going to be useful if I am going to keep Abbey safe and happy.

Goodwill Hunting

As we walk along the downtown streets, Abbey points out her favorite places.

"Have you ever been to this place?" she asks me, pointing to the Goodwill Store.

"I don't think so." There's usually a distinct smell of moth balls and death that makes me avoid resale shops.

Abbey's face is glowing with happiness.

"C'mon. I'll show you. I find a lot of really great stuff in here."

As we walk through the door, a tall, friendly man approaches us.

"Welcome to Goodwill. Can I help you ladies find anything?" Abbey looks smitten. I jump into mommy mode.

"No, thanks. My friend just wanted to show me your store."

"Yes, I know Abbey. She's one of our best customers. How are you?" They are both beaming at each other.

Abbey speaks up, "Good. My friend has never been here."

Mr. Goodwill gets a shocked look on his face and shakes his head. "Look around. We've got lots of new stuff."

Abbey struts toward the dress rack and I follow her casually. My goal is to watch her closely, but not to look like I am hovering.

"This looks like my mother's dress." She is staring at a brown dress with big white polka dots.

It probably is from her mother's era. I wonder if she thinks it actually belonged to her mother.

"I remember that she would get dressed up and she was really beautiful. My father was very handsome too. The women really liked him." Suddenly, I realize all this old, smelly stuff is triggering memories for Abbey.

As we walk through the store, she touches fabrics, and stories come pouring out. She is also collecting things she wants to try on. Some of them are dropping onto the floor. I offer to hold them, and she gladly hands them to me.

I notice some of the items are not even close to her size and some are outrageously expensive. With a twinge of guilt, I decide to purge some of the obviously unsuitable items. The wrong sizes are easy. As we move through the shop, I slip some of the items back onto racks as we pass them.

Abbey is still picking out clothes. I am filtering them and returning them discretely onto random racks. We are a shop keeper's nightmare. We are rearranging items from an organized system into a random kind of hide and seek game.

I remember reading about the Theory of Chaos, a philosophy that believes everything in the universe tends toward chaos. I tell myself, we are simply part of the chaos, furthering the process along. Occasionally, Abbey will circle around and find an item that I have hung back up. Sometimes, she will hesitate and then choose it again. If Abbey chooses the same item twice, I don't have the heart to discard it again.

We've moved into accessories. Abbey is modeling a purple hat with feathers. She is grinning as she admires herself in the mirror.

She hands a hat to me, "here, try this on."

"I look terrible in hats," I tell her as I plop it onto my head.

Abbey bursts out laughing. "Oh, that is awful" she says giggling.

I look into the mirror and cringe. "This is why the only thing I put on my head is a scrunchie."

Abbey thinks this is hilarious, "No one wears scrunchies."

"I have a whole collection," I tell her, "My favorite ones are pink and sparkly."

"I would never wear a scrunchie," she says laughing.

"That's why I wear them, because they are so uncool."

Finally, Abbey is ready to go to the fitting room.

"Do you want some help?" I ask her.

"No, I can do it myself."

I hand the pile of clothing to her, and she disappears behind the curtain. I pretend to be looking at items right next to her room. After a couple of minutes, her head peeks out.

"Will you help me with this stuff?"

The Secret Friend

"Of course, my daughter and I have a system to help each other try on clothes." She holds the curtain open, and I join her in the fitting room. She has not tried anything on and looks confused.

I reassure her, "If we do this together, it will be much easier."

"I want to try on my mother's dress first."

"Ok."

We work our way through the outfits. Each dress brings back a memory and demands a decision. She swivels around, watching her reflection intensely. As she evaluates the items, she says, "I like orange" or "that's too fancy" or "boring." Each time she chooses, she is remembering what she likes, who she is, and who she is not.

Based on her choices, she is bright, bold, colorful, artistic and a bit quirky. She is having fun trying on different identities. She has changed my opinion of Goodwill. Sometimes the best thing you can find at Goodwill is yourself.

Eventually, we make our way to Starbucks for coffee. I ask her what she would like to order. "I don't know. What are you having?"

I tell her my drink and she says, "Ok, I'll have the same thing." While I am paying for our drinks, Abbey walks over to a mother with a small child in a stroller. "He is so cute. What's his name?" she asks. The mother is smiling as she answers. I tell Abbey our drinks are ready. As we move away, Abbey tells me that she likes to say nice things about children, because it makes the mothers feel good.

"You've done your good deed for the day," I say admiringly.

Yeah, I like that." At that moment, her face is glowing. Helping someone else has made her feel useful.

Bird Droppings

I want to make sure Abbey arrives home safely, so I accompany her into her building. She fumbles with the keys a few times but manages to open the door. As we enter her apartment, a bird flies across the living room.

The sliding glass door to the balcony is still wide open.

A little scream comes out of my mouth, "Watch out. There's a bird in here!" I warn her.

"That's ok. He comes in here all the time."

She barely glances toward the panicked bird as she walks off into the kitchen. Her movement sends the bird flapping wildly down the hallway toward the bedroom. I can't leave her alone with a wild bird. I reluctantly follow the bird.

The bedroom appears to have been ransacked. Mountains of clothes are strewn about the room, mixed together with jewelry, magazines, rocks, potting soil, shoes, papers and photographs.

The bird is flailing against the window. Waving my arms, I try to guide the bird back toward the hallway just as Abbey walks through the bedroom door. The bird swoops desperately back across the room, crashes into the full-length mirror, and falls stunned to the floor.

"Oh, that's not good," she says, without emotion. She looks at me. "Do you have a pen?"

"A pen? Uh, no. Not on me."

"Ok," she says, nonchalantly. She is completely calm as she walks out of the room. I try to image how she is going to use a pen to get the bird out of the apartment.

The bird has recovered and flies toward the open closet. Getting the bird to fly down the hall, across the living room, and out the sliding glass doors is starting to seem impossible. There's only one small window in the bedroom, but at least it's the most direct route to freedom.

I climb over the mounds of stuff, push the screen out of the window, and watch it fall two stories to the ground. I circle back around the room and flap my arms like a crazy, tilting, windmill. I'm either going to save the bird or give it a heart attack.

Finally, some survival instinct kicks in and the bird flies out the open window. Abbey reenters the room with a piece of paper, but no pen. She hands the blank page to me. She doesn't seem to notice that the bird has left the building.

"So, how do I find you?" she asks smiling.

We walk back to the kitchen. I write my name and phone number down and stick the paper on the refrigerator door. I'm surprised she still hasn't asked about the bird.

"I had to push the screen out of the window, and it fell down into the courtyard. I hope that's all right, but it's the only way I could get the bird out of your bedroom."

She looks directly at me, "You worry too much. It's ok. John will get it. That's John's job."

The Secret Friend

I go home and write an email to John, telling him about our adventures. I explain why his bedroom screen is on the ground in the courtyard. Also, I mention our excursion to the Goodwill Store and his wife's shopping splurge. This is my first time I'm being paid for work in about 20 years. I wonder if I am going to get fired on my first day.

But John's response is as casual as Abbey's attitude toward the bird in the apartment.

"This is wonderful news!!! Thanks for pulling it off on your own. No worries. That bird comes into the apartment all the time. Abbey is impulsive, but shopping is her entertainment, so I am okay with it. She used to have good taste. You should plan to take her out again on Thursday."

Peace of Mind

Late that night, I sit at my computer, searching for options, solutions, and resources. The Alzheimer's Association offers a safe return bracelet for individuals who get lost and cannot remember how to get home, or even where home is located. For thirty-five dollars, it is peace of mind for the loved one.

I find cutting edge research and information on local researchers running clinical trials. I am filled with optimism as I discover a world of renowned scientists sharing hope and suggestions for improved quality of life for Alzheimer's patients. Support groups are abundant, and several are in our immediate neighborhood. Help is all around us, and I am feeling hopeful as I send all the links and suggestions to John.

I imagine he will be thrilled to learn of the available opportunities. I even offer to take Abbey to any appointments, doctors, or support groups. As I fall asleep, I anticipate John's joyous, appreciative response.

In the morning, I receive the following email from John. It is short and clear. "You should not get involved with providing solutions. You are already having a positive influence in what you are doing, so leave the organizing to me."

Abbey!

I show up at Abbey's apartment on Thursday morning and she is thrilled to see me.

"Would you like to get coffee?" I ask her.

"I'm ready to go."

We go to the Starbucks at the Stanford Mall. This seems to be a favorite spot for mommies and babies, and people walking their dogs. The baristas are friendly. When they ask Abbey her name, she tells them it is, "Abbey, like the Beatles, Abbey Road."

The barista behind the register looks at her, "Ah, Abbey. Like the long and winding road," he says breaking into song.

Abbey smiles at him, "Yup, that's me."

We carry our coffee outside the shop and take a front row seat to the parade of children and dogs passing in front of us. We are positioned perfectly to greet friendly people and pet furry creatures.

Abbey is so sweet with the children, playing little peek-a-boo games and sprinkling compliments on their mothers. Little dogs cozy up to her and she makes lovely comments to them as she rubs their necks.

"I had a Springer Spaniel," Abbey tells one dog owner, "her name was Maybelline."

I keep a checklist in my mind of all the positives of our experience. We are drinking coffee which researchers are saying is good for the mind, at least this week. John said she was not eating all day when she was alone. She is now eating banana bread with nuts. Abbey is out interacting with the world, which is more stimulating than sitting alone in her apartment. The encounters are bringing back memories for her. We are talking, laughing, and having fun. We are fulfilling the goal of being normal. Now, we need to add exercise.

"Have you ever been to the shoreline?" I ask Abbey.

"Yes, my father had a sailboat there," she says, "I used to go sailing with him all the time."

I think I remember hearing about a yacht club, but it is gone now.

"Would you like to go to the shoreline today? I have a bunch of bread I would like to feed to the ducks."

"I love feeding the birds. Let's go."

Our town scores extremely high on the politically correct scale. We are only allowed to feed the ducks at one particular pond. Warning signs are highly visible and prevalent. The stiff penalties mean the town is serious about enforcing this regulation.

When my children were little, we spent a lot of time around duck ponds. Feeding the birds is such a delightful activity. It's too bad someone had to change the rules. The last legal place to feed birds is the duck pond at the end of Embarcadero Road.

As Abbey and I get out of the car, the birds are already squawking. Several varieties of ducks and geese swim toward us.

Seagulls circle over our heads. We start tossing our bread. The more aggressive birds are hogging the food. Abbey wants the little, shy birds to get some bread. We come up with a strategy. I will throw some bread into the pond. While the aggressors are competing for the food, Abbey will throw some to the smaller, timid birds.

"We make a good team," I tell her.

"Yeah, I want to do this again," she says.

After the bread is gone, we walk over to a fenced area. Someone had the idea of creating a bird sanctuary and a breeding area for migrating species. Unfortunately, no one told the birds. For almost fifty years, the birds have flown by without noticing the special accommodations.

"I think last year was the first time the herons and egrets came here to breed" I tell Abbey, "It was so unusual that news teams were out here filming them."

"I used to see the birds when I came here with my father," Abbey says. "We had a poem we would say about the pelicans, but I can't remember it. Do you know it?"

"No, I don't think I do."

"I'll call John and ask him." She starts looking for her phone. I can't imagine any scenario where my husband would want me to call him at work and ask about a poem.

"Are you sure that John won't mind? You could ask him tonight." I suggest.

"John likes it when I call him." Abbey is holding her phone upside down and turning it over and over trying to remember how to use it. Finally, she hands me the phone. "I can't see the numbers very well. Will you dial it for me?"

"Of course, it's hard to see in this bright sunlight."

I open the phone and John's name is the first entry. I push the buttons and put the call on speakerphone. To my surprise, a happy voice answers the phone.

"Hi Abbey babe, what's shaking?" he says.

"I can't remember the poem about the pelican," she says, "Do you?"

"Sure. 'What a wondrous bird is the pelican. His beak can hold more than his belly can.' It's from Alice in Wonderland."

"Oh, yes, say it again." Abbey's face is glowing now as she and John recite the words together.

"Is Susan with you?" he wants to know.

"Hi, John. We are walking around the shoreline. I didn't know that poem and Abbey knew you would remember. I hope we're not bothering you."

"Of course not, call me anytime. I wish I was there with you. I'm so jealous," he says, "See you tonight. Bye."

"Ok, bye," she says.

"Abbey, I've seen pelicans here at the shoreline," I say.

"Let's go find them."

26

"Ok. That's so nice that John wants you to call him, even when he's working."

"Why wouldn't he want me to call?"

"Well, my husband never wanted me to bother him when he was at work."

"I wanted to ask you. Where is your husband?"

"We were married for 13 years and then we got divorced. He moved to Europe about a year ago."

"Why did you get divorced?"

"He and a friend of mine made a baby together."

"She doesn't sound like a very good friend."

"No, we're definitely not friends anymore."

"Do you have kids?"

"I have a boy and a girl. But they are pretty much grown up now."

"I wanted to have kids, but I couldn't. I wanted to adopt, but John's family said we couldn't. I'm really mad at his family. Do you want a new husband?"

"I suppose, but they're not that easy to find."

"I'll ask John tonight. He might have someone at work for you."

"Thanks."

"It's ok, he likes to be the hero," she says with exaggerated emphasis on "the hero."

"You're so funny."

"You know, I have Alzheimer's, but I think I'm getting better."

"I didn't know that, but I'm glad that you're getting better."

We are walking down a trail where I've seen the pelicans in the past. There's no sign of the pelicans, but a flock of painters has descended upon the shoreline. Abbey stares at one woman in particular. "I think I know her." As we walk closer, Abbey becomes more confident that the woman was a former neighbor.

"Hi, I think I know you," Abbey says to the woman.

The woman looks skeptical. "I don't think so."

"Where did you grow up?" Abbey wants to know.

"I'm not from around here. I just moved here about a year ago."

Abbey is still sizing her up. "Do you have any kids in the area?"

"No." The woman is not very friendly, and I think we should move on.

"Nice painting," I tell her.

"Thanks."

"Abbey, should we keep looking for the pelicans?" As we walk away Abbey says, "I'm pretty sure I know that woman."

28

We walk for a few more miles, but the pelicans seem to be hiding. I realize that it's probably time to bring Abbey back home. "Are you tired?" I ask her.

"No, I like walking, and we haven't found the pelicans yet."

"I think maybe the pelicans have moved south. It's too far to walk today, but we could look another day."

"Are you going to take me back to my dungeon?"

I feel guilty bringing her home, but I think John will be unhappy if we stay out too long.

"I'm sorry. I have to pick up my daughter today. Do you want to come back here again?"

"Oh, you have to go take care of your kids. Yes, we can come back again."

"Good, next time we will find the pelicans, and now I know the poem you taught me."

"Let's say it again," she says. Together we recite the pelican poem several times in hopes that at least one of us will remember.

We are almost at the car when Abbey spots a feather. "I have to get some of these," she says. She stoops down and starts picking up feathers.

"I just found a big one," I say, "Look, Abbey."

"That's nice. Look at this one."

Once, we start looking, we keep finding bigger and better feathers. Abbey starts picking up rocks as well. An hour later, we have an impressive collection of rocks, feathers, shells, and flowers. I give all of my findings to Abbey. She is surprised that I don't want to keep them.

"Would you like to put them in the back of the car?" I ask her.

"No, I want to hold them." All the way home, she keeps looking at the pieces of the shoreline sitting in her lap. Maybe these are breadcrumbs that lead back to the memories of the day.

We bring them upstairs to her apartment and arrange them on the dining room table. I thank her for walking the shoreline with me. As I start to leave, she reminds me, "We still need to find the pelicans, don't forget."

"OK, call me when you want to go," I tell her. I say this even as I know that we already have plans for our next get together.

Mixed Messages

After I drop Abbey off at her apartment, I call John to give him an update. He sounds thrilled. "You made a good start with Abbey, and I hope you want to continue. I am wondering if you want to keep this at two days a week or go for a third."

"I think it's going well. I would be happy to add another day."

"Ok, I will stop by on my way home to pay you. I'll buzz you around 6 p.m."

"Great. I've worked 7 hours this week."

John arrives at my apartment. I wonder if he feels as uncomfortable as I do. He says "good job" and hands me $70. I am embarrassed that I have to mention it, but I say seven hours times twenty dollars would be $140.

"Oh," he says, "I thought you said, seventy dollars." He reaches into his pocket and comes up with three more twenties. "Oops, that's all the money I have with me."

I decide that I will write down the amount from now on, since I do not like confrontation, or awkward interactions.

"I think that Abbey has really enjoyed our outings," I say.

John smiles, "This is one of those rare times when reality exceeds expectations." I think this is a compliment, but I wonder if there is a slight undercurrent of displeasure.

As much as I am delighted to describe our adventures and how delightful Abbey is, I am also aware that she is home alone while I am sitting here with her husband. We are discussing her behind her back. This is deception and I am not comfortable with it, even if it is a benevolent deception. I have to admit to John that I feel like we are co-conspirators, collaborating to deceive his wife.

"Abbey is desperate to feel normal. The magic is being included in the normal things of life," John says.

I understand the justification and I want to continue the arrangement. Still, part of me feels guilty for pretending and taking money to be her friend.

"Abbey is happy doing things with you," John says, "I'm really jealous of how much fun you're having."

I am seriously shocked that he would say this.

"In fact," John says, "maybe the three of us can go out and do something together."

I really can't picture this. "I think Abbey's preference is to be with you. I just fill in the spaces while you are at work," I tell John.

I also want to know what he thinks about taking Abbey to my chiropractor to get an adjustment and a massage. I have recently read that massage may be good for memory.

"You may have to help her get undressed and dressed again, but I will give her money to cover the cost."

"Do you want to take her, or maybe the two of you could go together?" I ask him.

"If I suggest it, she will refuse to go," he says. "You can try to get her to go, but I don't think she will want to. Also, if I mention it, she will know that we are talking to each other."

I am mortified. "I would never want her to find out that I wasn't her friend."

He shrugs, "She will figure it out eventually, but for now, I think it is better that she doesn't know that you are being paid."

I imagine how devastated she would be. "If she ever asks me if I'm being paid, I will deny it," I say adamantly.

He smiles, "Let's not worry about that now." As if on cue, his phone rings. He sees her picture and puts his finger to his lips as he answers her call. "Hi. I got stuck in traffic, but I'm just turning into the parking lot. OK. I'll be there in just a few minutes."

He covers the mouthpiece for the phone and whispers to me, "It's ok with me if you want to take her to the chiropractor, but I really don't think she will want to go."

He pulls a book out of his briefcase. "I highly recommend this book, 'Still Alice.' You might want to read it." And then, he walks out the door to hurry home to his wife.

A few minutes later, I get a text message from John, "I need coverage tomorrow starting at 10 a.m. Are you available? Abbey used to be a potter. You might go to the Artists Guild; they have a potter there. Her name is Joy."

"I'm available," I write, "I'll plan to be at your apartment at ten. The Artists Guild sounds like a good plan."

Joy to the World

The next morning, I walk over to Abbey's apartment and find her waiting on the balcony. "Hey, I was hoping you would come over today."

"Hi, I'm going out for coffee. Do you want to come with me?"

"Yes, I'm ready to go."

She comes bouncing out of the building. "I talked to John about finding a husband for you. He might know someone, but you need to lose some weight."

"Really? He's not exactly Brad Pitt," I think to myself. "Well, I will just have to get more exercise," I say.

"Do you want to help me?"

"Sure. You need to eat more salads like me."

We go back to the Starbucks at Stanford Mall and the same baristas are working. "Good morning, Abbey! What would you like today?" It's always nice to be recognized.

"I want the same thing again," she says in a flirty kind of voice.

"Got it. Mocha Latte for Abbey! With banana bread?"

"Yup." Abbey turns to me, "I like coming here a lot."

The Secret Friend

"Me too, everyone is so friendly and nice." Sometimes, routines can be comforting and easy. We even take the same seats and wait for the parade of people and pets to begin.

"Have you ever been to the Allied Arts Guild?" I ask.

"Oh, yeah. I know the potter there. Do you want to go there? I can introduce you to the artists." Abbey is pleased.

"Great. I've always wanted to meet the artists."

The Allied Arts Guild is nestled in a quiet residential area in Menlo Park. It is a walled colony of artists, gardens, and upscale shops. Artisans sell their jewelry, custom clothing, paintings, and other unique crafts. A restaurant is run by volunteers and the profits benefit the local children's hospital. Fountains and flowers dot the grounds, and it is all lovely in that colorful, posh, altruistic way.

Abbey guides me through the maze of flower beds, and a series of small, quaint buildings. We find the pottery shed out near the restored barn. The creaky door announces our arrival. The walls and tables are covered in unique, handmade items.

A white, lace curtain separates the showroom from another smaller room in back. We can see a pretty, dark haired woman busily working on her pottery wheel. She says hello but makes no effort to get up. Abbey calls to her and she reluctantly comes out to greet us.

"Hi. I brought my friend to see your stuff." It occurs to me that Abbey may not remember my name.

"Hi. I'm Susan. Your work is lovely."

"Thank you. I'm Joy."

Abbey picks up an expensive looking green bowl. I move closer as I watch her absentmindedly looking around.

"I have a bowl like this at home," she tells Joy. "Do you have any more?"

"More bowls?" she says with a tinge of impatience. I think Joy's personality may not match her name.

Abbey looks confused. I decide to jump into the conversation.

"Yes, do you have any more bowls like this in different sizes?"

"Just what's out here. But I can make any size you want."

I look at Abbey, "Do you want a particular size bowl?"

"No, I don't need any bowls. I have a lot at home."

Abbey looks over her glasses at me. She seems to be wondering why I would ask her such a bizarre question.

Her attention is drifting, and I gently take the bowl from her hands and set it back down on the shelf.

Joy looks back toward her pottery wheel, barely visible behind the swaying curtains. As Abbey's advocate, I consider the priorities. Joy's clay may be starting to harden, but she can get new clay. Abbey's neural circuits are beginning to harden, and practicing may help keep them fresh. I think Abbey's needs are more pressing.

Abbey asks how she made another piece of pottery. Joy's enthusiasm increases as she describes the process. They talk glazes and finishes, firing temperature and colors. Abbey is enjoying this mental exercise. These are the paths that lead back to her identity.

For the moment she is confident and knowledgeable. She is an equal in this world and her brain is cooperating by retrieving technical terms and obscure artistic bantering. In this moment, she is all there, whatever that means.

Joy brings her over to show her a shiny, gold necklace.

Abbey tells her excitedly, "My family came out west for the gold rush. My great-grandmother came to the United States from England. She took a girl from an Indian tribe in Maine, and they brought her to California to look for gold. My grandmother was really ugly, but they did really well. I have a lot of jewelry from them."

I'm trying to make sense of this story. Did her ancestors kidnap, or buy, or adopt an Indian child? Did they really bring her to California and make her pan for gold? Abbey is quite pleased with her family history. I look at Joy to see her reaction. Joy is talking about the inspiration for her work. I seem to be the only one who is concerned by the possible abduction story.

"This looks like my mother's jewelry." Abbey has picked up the gold necklace. She looks directly at Joy. "I used to have a lot more of her jewelry, but my husband is stealing it. He keeps giving it to his friends."

I have no idea what is true, but it might be time to let Joy get back to work.

"So, Abbey, should we go look at some more shops?"

"Ok, but I want to buy this first. How much is this?"

Joy takes the necklace and turns the tag over. I think she says one hundred and ten dollars. I'm starting to panic. Abbey opens her purse and digs around. She pulls out a twenty-dollar bill, a few one dollar bills, a couple of rocks, her house keys, and her grandfather's watch. "I hate this purse," she says for the first of a thousand times. She zips it closed, and then she unzips it again.

"We could come back and get it later," I suggest gently, hoping that she will forget.

"No, I want it now." Finally, she pulls out her credit card and hands it proudly to Joy. "I have money," she says as she signs her name on the dotted line. Joy smiles and tells us to come again.

Yikes, I think to myself. She can buy anything she wants.

Spanking Buddha in the Senior Center

We walk over to the art gallery. Abbey falls in love with a bold, bright orange photograph of Buddhist Monks. The framed print probably measures three feet by four feet. "I want to buy this," she tells the woman at the desk.

"Sorry, that's not for sale," the woman answers kindly. This is a huge relief, as I sense a kind of shopping tsunami. "If you like these photos, you might check out the Senior Center. I think the artist is showing some of her work over there."

"I think my father built the Senior Center," Abbey tells her. "He was a builder. Do you know him?"

The woman shakes her head, no.

"Maybe we should walk over to Senior Center," I suggest to Abbey. "We might find someone who knew your father." The Senior Center is only a mile away and exercise is good for us.

Abbey doesn't hesitate. "Let's go."

The Senior Center is known for its diverse, community programs. Maybe we will find something that will interest Abbey. We walk through the main entrance. A few silver haired gentlemen are reading newspapers and chatting pleasantly with each other. We ask if anyone grew up in the area and knew her family. She tells them her last name.

A man at one of tables says he graduated from the local college and thinks he knew her mother. He looks like he could have been a corporate CEO. He is wearing a long sleeve blue dress shirt and khakis. Abbey is thrilled and tries to remember her mother's name.

"My mother went to the same school. She was gorgeous," Abbey says enthusiastically.

"Oh, no," Mr. Corporate Khaki pants says, "the really attractive women are in Chicago."

A man sitting across from him disagrees. "How can you say that? The most beautiful women are in California."

"No, the women in Chicago are strong and they don't take any bullshit. If you do something wrong, they slap you. If you do something very bad, they might even give you a spanking," he says grinning.

"Seriously?" I'm thinking. He looked so proper and normal.

Abbey looks at me, "I don't like this place."

"Let's check out the garden," I quickly guide her away from the table where the men are now starting to raise their voices with each other.

A small Asian man comes over to us and says hello. "My name is Hung, like Hungry." He smiles and rubs his belly. "I take care of the garden."

"Hi, I'm Abbey."

"Hi, I'm Susan. My friend, Abbey loves to grow flowers."

"Maybe you can help me in the garden," he tells her.

"Yes, I want to get a job again," she says.

"Abbey, what kind of plant is this?" Hung asks.

"Agapantha," she says without hesitation.

"Should I trim it back now or later?" he asks. She stares at the plant and then reaches for a different one.

"I don't know." She seems confused.

Hung tries again, "Come, look at the roses. Do I need to do anything with them?"

"These are different from the ones I worked with," she says.

I pull a branch down. "Oh, Abbey, smell this."

She sniffs the rose and smiles, "Odiferous."

"Odiferous? What does that mean?" I ask.

"It means they have a strong smell." She is very pleased now.

Hung says to her "You can come and help me in the garden any time you want. Ok?"

"OK."

"Hey, Abbey, you just got a job," I say.

"Yeah, I got a job. I like that. Wait, 'til I tell John. I got a job today."

We walk around the facility and check out the listings on the bulletin board. I look for classes that would be fun and appropriate for Abbey. I notice a flyer for Zumba.

"Abbey, would you like to try this class? It's dancing and music."

"Ok, I like dancing and music," she says.

I pull a couple of flyers off the wall. "The next class is on Tuesday."

"Ok, remember to pick me up."

After I drop Abbey off at her apartment, I send John an email to let him know what we have done today. This way if Abbey does not remember, he can ask questions that will prompt her memory. I tell him I would like to take Abbey to Zumba on Tuesday.

John responds to my email. "Going to the Senior Center was brilliant. Did she tell you that her father built the Senior Center? I think it's true. I will have her dressed for Zumba on Tuesday."

Chapter 3 February

What's Stuff Got to Do with It?

The following morning, I can hear the yelling before I even reach their door. She is in tears, and he is frustrated. She's wearing bright purple pants, a man's multicolored striped shirt, orange socks, and one shoe on the wrong foot. The other shoe is missing.

"I told her she needs to change her shoes," he says angrily. I watch her remove the shoe, and then put in back on the wrong foot again.

"Leave me alone," she says, "Get out of my apartment." She is mad, too.

I remember coping with these issues when my kids were young. I would ask myself if the battle was worth fighting, or if this was the hill I wanted to die on. When my daughter was in the princess phase, a fluffy little pink swirl and sparkly tiara accompanied me everywhere I went.

I've been seen in public with Ninja turtles, dancers with tutus, skater dudes, and a tiny version of my mother complete with a gray wig. I was a little freaked out when my daughter was dressing up as a mini-me imitation of my mother.

Eventually, I learned to go with the flow. I'm not sure why he cares so much about her clothing choices. Given all the obstacles and difficulties they are facing, clothing seems insignificant.

Perhaps he wants to maintain the façade that everything can still be the same if she looks the same. I wonder if he always decided what she would wear. Perhaps the stress of watching his independent wife regress into someone who needs help eating and dressing is a painful reminder of things he cannot control.

Alzheimer's has changed their dynamic from equal partners to more of a parent child relationship. Maybe this makes both of them sad and angry.

"You stole my shoes, just like you stole all my other stuff," she accuses him. "I want my stuff."

"Where's all this stuff?" I ask him.

"It's in storage. We don't have room for it here," he explains impatiently.

"I want it now. My father gave me his stuff and it's special to me. I think you just gave it all away."

"I need to go to work," he says, "I'm not going to discuss this right now."

"Is there anything I can do to help get the stuff?" I interject delicately.

"No, I have to contact the storage place, but I have been too busy."

He storms out the door, and she is left crying on the couch.

"He doesn't want a wife with Alzheimer's," she says, and I can feel my heart breaking for her.

44

"I'm sure he loves you. He's probably having problems at work." She is looking at me for comfort, and I'm willing to make up anything to help her feel better.

"Do you think so?"

"Of course," I say, "I'm sure he would rather be home with you."

"It's just a stupid job with a crappy company. He should just quit and stay home with me." She is shaking her head in frustration.

"Maybe he has to work because he needs the money or health insurance. I don't know. Maybe you can talk about it with him tonight."

This seems to appease her, at least temporarily. "I'll ask him tonight. But I still want my stuff."

"Well, he said the stuff is in storage. I can ask him about it again, if you want me too."

Now she looks hopeful. "Yes, I liked that you asked him about my stuff. You can keep asking him about it."

"Ok, I will do whatever I can to help you get your stuff." I am hoping this resolves the issue at least for the moment. But now that she has enlisted me, I am wondering, what's this stuff and where is it?

"Do you want to go get coffee?" she asks me.

"I would love to get coffee." I say enthusiastically. I am thrilled that we have established our morning ritual.

"Hey, you need another shoe. I'll help you look for it and then we can go to Starbucks."

"It might be under my bed," she says hopefully. The bedroom still looks like tornadoes have blown through and upended everything. We get down on our hands and knees and start pulling clothes, towels, books, jewelry, rocks, and finally shoes out from under the bed. We find two matching shoes and she happily agrees to wear them.

"I got these from Nordstrom's on sale. They liked me so much they said I only had to pay five dollars." The shoes are from an expensive designer and I'm not sure how she could have bought them so cheaply.

"I like the color a lot." They are bright red, leather flats, a bit eccentric-looking and bold. She is admiring her feet as she twirls them around. They are her ruby red slippers; I hope they contain some special magic for her.

You Crack Me Up

Getting out of the house has been an emotional rollercoaster this morning. I can tell she is still brooding about the events. When we finally emerge from the building, I stop and look up at the gorgeous blue sky.

"It's a beautiful day. Look at that perfect blue sky. Let's take a deep breath and release all the stress in our bodies."

Abbey goes along with it and starts breathing deeply and soulfully. She closes her eyes and flutters her arms.

"Listen to the birds singing," I say, "Let's just be happy like the birds."

She looks at me smiling and we both start waving our arms and giggling. We are silly birds, we are leaving the stress far behind, as we start our daily migration toward the happy place.

We get into my car and head out for today's adventure. I am the maker of magic. I need to make sure we end up at certain places on time, but make it look spontaneous. I have booked Abbey's chiropractic treatment and massage for today.

Starbucks has another location a few doors away from our destination. After a leisurely coffee and friendly interaction, I suggest a walk down to see my friend, Dr. Bill. I have explained to Dr. Bill and the staff that Abbey has Alzheimer's, and she may not even come inside. I can make the plans, but Abbey will decide whether she wants to participate.

The office is bright and visible through large glass windows from the outside. Dr. Bill comes over and gives me a warm, wonderful bear hug.

"Sometimes I come here just for the hugs," I say laughing. "Abbey, this is my friend, Dr. Bill. Would you like a hug too?"

Abbey opens her arms and smiles at Dr. Bill, and he wraps his arms around her gently. "Hey, how would you like an adjustment and a massage?" he asks Abbey.

"I'd like that," she answers quickly.

"Great, come on back," he says. Dr. Bill leads the way, this could not have been easier.

Dr. Bill helps Abbey up onto the table. Even though she is only sixty-two years old, her body is often rigid and inflexible. I'm worried about her falling off the table, but Dr. Bill stays close to her. He pulls and tugs and bundles her up in his arms and cracks her back. I am impressed with her willingness to cooperate and change positions. By the time he has finished the adjustment, she is grinning with delight.

"I like this a lot. I'm going to tell my husband, so he can have this too."

"Great. Would you like to have a massage?" Dr. Bill asks her.

"Oh, yeah, I love massages," she says. Dr. Bill takes us over to meet the masseuse. I have already spoken to her. She knows that Abbey might need help getting undressed and dressed.

"I'll wait out here by the magazines," I tell them. Abbey is already walking away. She looks taller and straighter. I will sit outside the room if any problems arise.

After an hour, Abbey emerges from the room with a dreamy, contented look on her face.

"I'm definitely coming back to have more massages," she tells me. I am relieved and delighted to see her so relaxed and happy. "I'm bringing John back here," she says, "Can you write down the name of this place, so I can tell him about it?"

"Of course," I say.

The receptionist gives us a brochure with the phone number and address. I have paid for the appointment, but Abbey mentions nothing about paying. We say goodbye to everyone. It has been a success. Abbey tells them she will be back, and she will bring her husband with her.

No New News is Old News

The next morning, I drive over to Abbey's apartment. She is standing on her balcony. When she sees me, she starts waving, "I'll be right down." A few minutes later she appears with her keys and purse. She is eager to get going.

We get into the car. Abbey tells me she loved the massage, but she's not going back to Dr. Bill again. I'm surprised.

"I thought you were going to take John for a massage," I say.

She shakes her head, "John was mad about the money and anyway this is John's job. John is going to give me massages now."

I choose a different Starbucks location for coffee this morning. As we make our way through the crowd, Abbey approaches a distinguished looking man reading the newspaper and drinking his coffee.

"Hi. I think I know you." I wait for his reaction, before I intervene.

"Abbey! How are you?" I am relieved and happy to hear his response.

Abbey is beaming. "I'm good. How is Sally?

"She is doing well," he says.

He looks over at me, "Hi, I'm Peter. My wife, Sally, worked with Abbey at the local newspaper." His English accent is disarming, and he seems genuinely pleased to see us.

50

The Secret Friend

He asks Abbey if she has seen the new offices. "You must go over and say hello to your friends. Louisa is still there. I'm sure she will give you a tour of the new building. It's very impressive."

Abbey is filled with confidence. "Ok, I will. Please say hello to Sally, ok?"

Peter wraps his arms around Abbey, "It was wonderful to see you. I'll tell Sally you asked for her."

He nods "Nice to meet you, Susan. Hope to see you again." He must know about Abbey's condition, but there is no indication of it in this interaction.

"I would love to go over to the newspaper," I tell Abbey, after we finally find a place to sit. "Would you like to go over to the Almanac after we finish our coffee?"

She is enthused about the idea. Visiting places and people from the past will help stimulate memories.

"Ok, I'm ready to go." She places her empty cup on the table. I take this as a sign that she is eager to see her former colleagues.

It only takes a few minutes to find the building. Just before we get to the fancy new steel structure, Abbey stops to study the brown, wooden church next door.

"I think my father built this church," she says looking at the steeple. "He wasn't religious, and he didn't care what kind of church it was, he just liked building them."

We read the plaque next to the front door, but it is just a welcome sign, with no historical information.

"My father used to take me to work with him," she says, "I think I remember coming here."

As I watch her trying to interpret her thoughts, I realize that having Alzheimer's must be similar to being in a constant state of déjà vu. Something feels familiar, maybe you've been there before, maybe not, or maybe one thing reminds you of something else. I try to imagine how confusing the world must appear when you cannot trust your thoughts.

Abbey keeps looking back at the church as we walk toward the newspaper. We push through the glass doors. Abbey asks the receptionist if her friend, Louisa, is working.

Within a minute, Abbey's friend comes bounding down the stairs, thrilled to see her. We are escorted up to the newsroom and Louisa is overjoyed to see Abbey.

The publisher comes out of his office and Abbey greets him by name. They are excited to show off the new computers and fancy magnetic wall. Abbey remembers working in the design department. She asks about a few other people, but most of her former coworkers have left the newspaper.

They reminisce about some funny incidents, but I notice Abbey's interest is fading. She walks over to a window, where she can see the church next door.

"I think my father built that church," she tells them. "Do you know anything about that church?" she asks Louisa. Unfortunately, no one has any information on the building.

The Secret Friend

"But it looks old," Louisa offers helpfully, "I think your father might have built it. He was a very good builder."

Louisa looks at me sadly. Abbey is lost in thought as she stares out the window. It is time to go. We promise to visit again. On the way out, I grab a couple of newspapers as tangible reminders of our visit.

I send John an email telling him how fortuitous it was that we should meet Peter, and how Abbey's friends gave us a tour of the newspaper offices.

"Yes, you've done a great job at following the threads. Have you had a chance to read Still Alice, yet?"

More is Better

Abbey is so enthusiastic about our adventures that John keeps adding days to our schedule. We agree that I will take Abbey out five days a week for approximately seven hours a day. This means I need to find interesting, appropriate, engaging activities, which appear spontaneous, will be mentally and physically stimulating, and still act like a couple of friends out having fun.

Also, I need to keep the cost of the activity in mind. Some days, when I bring Abbey home, she will ask me to remind her of what we did that day. How much money should we spend if she doesn't remember? Who can tell what she remembers, or what makes a difference? If she does not have long to live, how much is too much?

I send John an email, "I was wondering if taking photos of our adventures would be helpful to Abbey. She mentioned that she was a photographer, and she would like to use a camera again."

His response is positive, "Good thought. Abbey used to have a Hasselblad. I'll look into getting her a camera."

"Great. Although, I wouldn't pay a lot for a camera. Maybe we just want to get a disposable camera. We can take pictures of the places we visit, and they can help Abbey remember where we've gone and what we've done," I write in response.

The Secret Friend

I'm thinking how difficult it is to keep track of the keys, cell phone, purse, credit card, any items of clothing, and Abbey. I don't want to worry about an expensive camera, too.

"Ok. I will pick up a couple of disposable cameras. Try to get some signage in the photo," he writes, "We like signage."

Garden-gate

Knowing that Abbey was a botanist, I think she would enjoy a visit to Filoli House and Garden. When I mention this, she is excited about going to see the flowers. Filoli has a wonderful reputation for spectacular gardens.

I drive up to the guardhouse at the entrance to the property. The guard tells us we will each have to pay $15 to see the gardens. I have no idea how long Abbey will be interested in walking around and looking at the gardens, or if she will even remember. I ask if we can just pay $15 because we might not stay long. I do not want to mention the disease. He says we have to pay the full amount, or we cannot go in.

Abbey says, "Never mind. Let's go home."

Going home is not an option, but I cannot say this to Abbey. I always have alternative plans if the first idea does not work out. I tell the guard that we do not want to pay $30. Cars are waiting impatiently behind me. I ask if I can drive down the road to turn around. He waves me through the gate, and we drive down the narrow road to the main parking area.

Once we reach the parking lot, Abbey says, "I'm glad we came here. I really wanted to see the gardens."

I cringe. "I didn't pay the guard. That means we would be sneaking into the gardens."

"That will make it more fun," she says.

The Secret Friend

I look at her face, she is grinning mischievously. What's the worst that could happen?

I give in. "Alright. If they catch us and throw us in jail, we'll have to call John to come and bail us out." She likes this whole idea. We are Butch Cassidy and the Sundance Kid of the garden set.

We avoid the main entrance and hop on a path as though we have been strolling around the grounds. The plants are conveniently labeled, so we take turns reading the names out loud to each other.

One name tag has fallen to the ground, we go over and pick it up. As we are standing in front of the bush, I see a couple of women with official looking badges walking briskly toward us. We do not have name tags, and I think we are about to be busted. Who breaks into a garden?

One of the women is calling to us, "Excuse me. Excuse me! Hello!" Abbey and I stand next to each other like two naughty children facing the school principal. "You two need to get off the grass. Didn't you see the signs?"

Relief sweeps over me, "Of course, sorry, we were just fixing the name tag on this plant," I say.

Suddenly, they are nice to us, "Oh, we didn't realize that. Sorry. Thank you for doing that. Enjoy the gardens."

As they walk away, Abbey beams at me as though we have pulled off a major heist. We wander through the gardens, but the flowers are anticlimactic. Abbey is still enjoying our rebellious entry.

"We broke into the gardens, didn't we?"

"Yes, we did."

"I like that."

Abbey notices the gift shop and wants to go in. One of the volunteers comes over and we ask her endless questions. We tell her that Abbey is a botanist. The volunteer also grew up locally and thinks she remembers Abbey's family.

I watch Abbey interact with this stranger and I would never suspect she had Alzheimer's. It's as if she can sometimes shut off the disease. Abbey buys seeds, a plant, and a book about flowers.

The Gardens have been good to us, and I even buy a floral scarf, as a thank you contribution.

Grow Your Own

That night, as I am searching through the local events and activities near us, I find an article about a community garden at Stanford University. I think this would be another interesting adventure for us. If we could get a small plot of land, we could grow our own vegetables and flowers. This would satisfy Abbey's desire for a garden and give her a sense of accomplishment. Perhaps working with the soil and plants will keep her mind active. I decide to make the community garden tomorrow's theme.

The next day, I mention planting a garden to Abbey, and she loves the idea. While we sip our coffee, we talk about what we want to plant. I'm thinking about tomatoes, cucumbers, and pumpkins, but Abbey is only interested in growing flowers. I'm surprised, but we will have plenty of room to grow it all, we just need to find it first.

I have deliberately not looked for the exact location of the garden. Our mission today will be to walk through the Stanford campus until we find the community garden. We start at one end of the campus and for the next eight hours we take the deluxe tour. We saunter through buildings and admire the architecture. We discover a spectacular gem display in the earth science building. We pose with the figures in the sculpture garden.

Our destination gives us a reason to talk to students, professors, and other people wandering around on the campus. Many people have heard about the community garden, no one knows exactly where it is located. I imagine we are on an adventure to find the Wizard of Oz, without the flying monkeys (I hope). Finally, we trudge through metal gates toward a couple of greenhouses, and what looks like the most promising location for a garden.

We walk tentatively by a field of corn on one side and green beans on the other. Flowers are blooming everywhere, and I wonder if we have encountered the illusive, community garden. A tall, handsome man walks out of a small building toward us. He's about our age and has a calm, quiet air about him. He is part mountain man, professor, and farmer. I wonder if he will evict us from the property for trespassing.

He introduces himself as Ray. We tell him that we are looking for the community garden. He thinks it may just be down the street. Suddenly, a rooster appears and lets out a huge screeching noise.

Abbey becomes very excited. "I had a rooster named Ramon. Is that your rooster?"

"That rooster just showed up here one day, I think someone just dropped him off, so I decided to get some chickens for him," he says, "Do you want to see the chickens?"

Ray leads the way across the grounds to the greenhouse. Abbey is telling Ray about her chickens and goats. I'm looking around for any sign of another human being and wondering if we should be more cautious. I hope this is not the farm-equivalent of the "come over here and see my puppy."

The Secret Friend

We enter a greenhouse. Chickens are hopping and flying all around us. Ray tells us he ordered a dozen and plans on keeping them for eggs and will eventually make chicken stew out of them. I glance at Abbey to see if this upsets her, but she is mesmerized by Ray.

"How did you get this job?" I ask Ray.

"I like to grow things. C'mon, I'll show you my roses."

Again, we are following Ray through a maze of greenhouses, down a path of joyous color, and find ourselves in front of some of the most perfect roses I have ever seen.

Ray tells us how he would win prizes for his roses, but mostly because he lived in a place that corresponded perfectly with the timing of the competition. I add modesty to his growing list of appealing traits. He has rare specimens, and Abbey and I enjoy smelling each one of the perfumed flowers.

Ray offers to show us an unusual fruit tree. He is charming and patient. He takes out his knife and slices the fruit and we are literally eating out of his hands. I have no idea what I am eating, but the fruit is juicy and delicious. Maybe, we have stumbled into some enchanted garden, and we are eating forbidden fruit. He offers us another slice of mystery fruit and we are quick to indulge. He brings us over to another tree and cuts off some grapefruit.

"Come back any time and take as much as you want," he offers. By now, Abbey and I are enamored with this gentle cultivator of all things lovely and yummy.

Ray tells us that he used to live by the ocean and loved to sail in all kinds of weather.

"Abbey's husband is a sailor," I say, "Maybe you could go out on his boat together."

I do think people drop into our lives for a reason. Abbey says she liked to sail with her father, but she doesn't sail with John because it's too cold on his boat. We decide to exchange phone numbers and Abbey is eager to tell John about Ray. As we are leaving, Ray cuts some flowers for us to take home. He says we are welcome to visit whenever we like.

As soon as we walk away, Abbey turns to me, "If anything happens to John, I'm going for Ray. He's a keeper."

I laugh, but Abbey is serious. "Really, he can grow things and take care of himself."

I agree with her. "I should be looking for a husband like Ray," I say.

Abbey nods her head. "Yes, my father always told me to 'find a man who will carry you out of a burning building.'"

I think this is excellent advice. "I think Ray would carry you out of a burning building, cover you with rose petals, and feed you enchanted berries," I tell her.

She stares at me. She is not kidding around. "If you don't want him, then I do."

Sleeping Around

John sends me an email about the upcoming weekend. "Hey, I got in touch with your friend, Ray. I would like to go sailing with him on Saturday. Can you take Abbey out for the day?"

"Sorry, I'm moving this weekend. But I'm only moving to the next building. This apartment has gotten too expensive. I'm downsizing from a two bedroom to a one-bedroom apartment. I'm going to put my son in the bedroom. I'm going to be sleeping on the sofa for a while."

"Ok. I'm thinking of sleeping on my boat next weekend. Would you be able to watch Abbey from Friday morning until Saturday evening? I don't think she needs you to sleep over, just get to our apartment early on Saturday morning. She should be able to stay alone for one night. She might need help dressing and you need to have meals with her, or else she won't eat. Let's see if we can make this happen." I cannot imagine anyone leaving her home alone. But he has already decided he needs to do this.

My son and I spend the weekend moving our things from the old place to the new place. I'm surprised to see how much we have accumulated. The move takes more time and energy than I expected. The unpacking will just have to be done over time. Monday morning comes, and Abbey and I are back to our routine.

Over the week, John and I email each other with concerns and suggestions.

I send several emails to John asking for information. "Given Abbey's level of difficulty and confusion, I think it would be prudent to make a list of contact persons, names of doctors, list of medications, physical descriptions, allergies, and any other information, in case of emergency."

"Sure, I've been meaning to put something together," he emails back.

Just before his departure, John sends me the requested information and some comments:

"The major issues I predict are as follows:

"1. She will not be able to get dressed in the morning.

"2. She will not eat alone.

"3. If she uses the microwave, the breakers might blow, and all lights will go out. She does not know how to fix this.

"4. If she is really tired, she will forget how to use her phone and be unable to make a phone call.

"5. Under some conditions, she will wander and get lost and might forget her keys. She does know how to go to the administrative office to get help, and she is known to the security guards, so this is manageable (so far).

"6. If she goes out by herself, she might lose her pocketbook, credit card and/or cell phone. I have always been able to retrieve her pocketbook by back-tracing where she went as she will remember bits and pieces of where she went. She has lost her cell phone several times. She has lost her credit card once. Otherwise, the credit card has always shown up somewhere in the apartment eventually.

"7. In the worst-case scenario, she should be wearing a Medical Alert bracelet, but she has refused in concept to do this. Linda, her sister, told me in an email today that she has ordered one for Abbey, so this is pending. The next best option was mentioned by a friend, getting a tattoo, informally, along with some girlfriends. I am not certain what the tattoo should say, but some identifier like name and social security number might be appropriate.

"I will tell the administrative office that you have my permission to access our apartment, as needed. Also, I am copying Abbey's sister, Linda, on this email. I have included Linda's contact information; in case you need to reach her."

The reality of her impairment is sobering, and honestly, a bit frightening. I may not have fully grasped the level of responsibility this job would require. Keeping her safe will entail an extra amount of vigilance.

I understand that desperate scenarios demand desperate measures or something like that. But, still, in what world would tattooing someone's social security number on their body be acceptable? I'm trying to imagine a conversation where we tell Abbey that because she won't agree to wear a bracelet, we're going to get our social security or phone numbers tattooed on our, hands or foreheads? Perhaps in the world of Alzheimer's, the outrageous starts to seem plausible.

A Different Perspective

Soon after, I receive a thoughtful and exquisitely written email from Abbey's sister, Linda. She is kind, appreciative, and enlightening. She applauds my efforts and John's dedication to her sister.

"Abbey and I are less than two years apart, and in the big picture, we are very different. In the details—how we talk, what catches our attention, our strong moral compasses, we are similar.

The Abbey you know is not the sister I knew for fifty years. This is a big problem for me. I loved the sister I had. I resent that she has changed. I try very hard to be kind, inclusive, and generous. It is a struggle.

Examples: The childlike wonder that sparks Abbey's new personality either didn't exist before or was hidden. Another example, she was basically an introvert, not the extrovert you see now.

Abbey was caustic, articulate, not particularly interested in the things most women revere or revel in. She was artistic, dependent yet not mousy, unconcerned with others, never a joiner. She had a sharp edge, enjoyed defying convention, and didn't mind telling you what she thought, even if it might crush you. I couldn't take her in large doses, but I loved her in small ones.

Abbey's disease... I am for anything that might help.

Lastly, I love John. I am grateful to him for his devotion to my sister, his unwavering patience and kindness. I support anything he may do for himself. I want him to sail, to play tennis, to enjoy meals with friends. His sacrifice is enormous. I appreciate your giving him the gift of time and relief, knowing that when you are with Abbey, she is safe. Thank you."

I am astounded by this new perspective. This is a version of history that I could not have imagined. I write back to her immediately.

"Linda, Abbey is lucky to have such a wonderful sister who cares so much. I will tell you a little about me. I have a BA in psychology, worked for a newspaper, married a professor from Brown University, moved to New Jersey for five years, and have two wonderful children.

My husband was the founder of a pharmaceutical start-up searching for novel antibiotics. We owned a home, and I was fortunate enough to stay at home with my kids and volunteer in the schools. I started a food program at the elementary school making healthy, hot food available to all students and feeding the disadvantaged kids for free.

My husband and I divorced, resulting in devastation for our children. There is a long, painful, version, but I will stick to just the basic facts here. My husband had our house sold by court order. He later told me that the stockbroker refused to sell my stock when I asked him to, due to "pressure from the principals in the company." The company went bankrupt. I lost everything in that company and due to some creative financial maneuvering by many of the same people, my 500,000 plus shares in another company, were declared worthless.

I'm trying desperately to stay in this area to remain close to my children. Abbey often asks about my life, and I give her the uncomplicated version.

I hope I am bringing something positive to Abbey's life. When she expresses an interest in an area, I research options on the internet and try to find places that she will enjoy and activities where she will succeed. I frame our outings as adventures, and we try to find a purpose in every day. Please share any ideas or suggestions for activities that she might enjoy."

I'm glad that Abbey's sister and I have established a relationship, but the time for reflection is limited. The plans for John's respite have been made and Friday morning arrives quickly. It is now up to me to keep Abbey safe, engaged, and happy until John returns.

Show Time

I show up at Abbey's apartment and ask her if she would like to get coffee. John tells the story of how he is going to sleep on his boat, and I act surprised as if I am hearing this for the first time.

"Great," I tell Abbey happily, "we can go out and have some fun."

"If you're going on your boat, I want some money," Abbey demands.

"Why don't you and Susan go out for dinner tonight? Here's some money, maybe you can even go to the movies and out to dinner."

"Maybe," she says, her hand still outstretched. "I think I need more money," she says, without even looking at how much he has given her. He gives her a couple more twenties and she does a little happy dance.

"Where's my purse?" We all start looking for the purse, playing our parts perfectly. I have no idea if the money will make it into the purse.

I have decided to use one of my favorite parenting techniques. We will play until we are totally exhausted and then drop into bed for a good night's sleep. We make our regular stop at Starbucks and then we are off to the California Academy of Sciences in San Francisco. As we travel up the highway, clouds of fog are drifting over the majestic mountains. I put on the soundtrack from the Sound of Music, and we are singing "The Hills are Alive with the Sound of Music."

We are feeling good, and I am optimistic about the next thirty-six hours.

We drive around the circle of museums and Abbey points to the de Young Museum of Art. "My grandmother and grandfather worked there, and they wrote a book about art for children. I used to go to that museum all the time."

I wonder if this is the same grandmother that was stolen from the Indian tribe, or maybe a different one. I decide not to ask.

"I've never been there. Would you like to go today?" I am happy to let her choose, in fact, I think it makes our arrangement seem more natural.

"No, I've already seen it too many times," she says, "Let's go to the science museum." As we enter the museum, she says, "Oh, I've been to this place before, too."

"Good, you can show me around. But first I have to go to the bathroom."

"Ok, but you really need to see a doctor, you have to go to the bathroom a lot."

Abbey never asks to go to a bathroom, but she will always use the toilet once we are there. So, to be safe, we go quite often. Going to the public restroom can be challenging. I have come up with several techniques for this occasion. Most recently, I try to get two stalls together and then I talk to her so that I know that she has not left the room.

Sometimes, she gets "locked in" and cannot open the door. She will turn the handle and forget to push the door. When she says she can't get out, I coach her outside the door to turn the knob. I keep pushing or pulling discretely until the door opens and she is free. We do this quite often. It's just a normal part of how we do things.

Usually, we are laughing, and I am repeating some version of my rant about how someone keeps changing everything in the bathrooms just to keep us thinking.

"When did going to the bathroom turn into an IQ test? How am I supposed to know if I need to flush the toilet, or if the toilet wants to flush itself? Why do some sinks have faucets and handles, and some sinks make you do the wave dance until they spit out a tiny trickle of water?

"Why is every soap dispenser different? Am I supposed to push down on the pump, press the lever on the wall mount, or let my hand hover in just the right spot to get a tiny squirt of soap?

"Why is it so hard to dry my hands? I have to locate the motion detector on the tug-less paper towel machines that almost always refuse to work. Sometimes I have to push a button for a blast of hot air or plunge my hands into some device that looks like a toaster, or a microwave. By the time I've completed the mental gymnastics of the bathroom puzzle, I'm ready to take a nap."

This always makes Abbey laugh and makes our confusion seem normal.

Suddenly, as we are standing at the sink, Abbey turns to me and asks me the dreaded question, "Did John tell you to take me here?"

"What?" I'm shocked. "Of course not. You and I decided to come here."

"Is John paying you to take me here?"

I think my heart has stopped beating and I'm thinking of all the ways this could go wrong.

"John pay me? Why would John pay me? Look how hard it is for you to get money from John," I say, laughing nervously. "He is certainly not going to give me any money."

This makes her laugh. "You're right. He is so cheap."

The horrible moment has passed, and I have lied to her, just as I told John I would. I wonder what would prompt her to ask me that now.

"Are you going to show me around the science museum?" I ask. I hope we have resolved the issue.

"Yes, c'mon, there's a lot of stuff to see."

For the next couple of hours, she points at fish and alligators and tells me to look at them. We walk through the rain forest exhibit, where colorful parrots squawk and butterflies flutter around our heads.

The Secret Friend

People are friendly and we find ourselves talking with other visitors about the strange and beautiful sights around us. This is our optimal environment. We are living in the moment, appreciating all that is around us, socializing, taking in all the sights, and exercising our bodies, and our minds.

"Hakuna Mata." I say. "It means be happy." I am taking some liberty with the translation.

She laughs, "Hakuna Mata. I like that."

A couple of people nearby overhear us and start singing along, "Hakuna Mata." Then we're all giggling and dancing in the jungle.

We are still in good spirits as I drive us back home.

Abbey is hungry, "Let's go to that place we went to before, you know the one?" I think she must be getting tired if she cannot remember the name of the restaurant. Now, I need to guess what she is thinking.

"Buck's?" I ask hopefully.

"Yeah, let's go to Buck's." Buck's is a popular place. Venture capitalists mingle with rock stars, and technology millionaires. The restaurant is decorated with funky, unusual, and bizarre kitsch, artifacts, and art.

I think Abbey enjoys the cool atmosphere.

Buck's is busy, as usual. I look around. Neil Young is sitting at one of the tables. I love his music and suddenly I am awestruck being so close to him. I tug on Abbey's arm and whisper, "Abbey, look, I think that's Neil Young, the singer."

Abbey is unimpressed, "Yeah, I've seen him here a bunch of times. Let's get some beer." Abbey is so nonchalant, and I am so uncool. I keep looking over at Neil Young, but I'm too shy to approach him.

Bedtime Stories

We eventually arrive home around 10 p.m. Abbey seems tired, and I help her bring her things inside and get her settled. "John's staying on his boat tonight, but he will be home tomorrow night," I say, "I can stay with you if you want."

"No, you don't need to do that. I'm ok," Abbey says. Before I leave, I make sure that her cell phone is plugged in and charging, and the lights are on in her bedroom and bathroom.

"I'll be back in the morning, and we can go out to breakfast, ok?"

"I'm fine. I'll see you in the morning." I give her a hug and she closes the door behind me.

I get home and collapse on the couch. I'm exhausted, but I need to get some sleep, because I want to get back to her apartment early. Tomorrow is my birthday, but I've already told my kids that I am not available to celebrate because I'm working.

I'm just crawling under the covers when my cell phone rings. Abbey is sobbing and I can't understand what she is saying.

"Are you still at home?" I think she says 'yes'. "I'm coming right over. Just wait for me," I tell her. I get dressed again and run over to her apartment.

She opens the door, and she looks terrified. Tears are streaming down her face.

"Why would he leave me alone? I have a disability. If I had a husband who had a disability, I wouldn't leave him home alone."

I put my arms around her. "You're okay now." I have never heard her talk so openly or honestly about her disease.

"I shouldn't be alone. He should be here with me." She looks so small and helpless.

"I can stay with you," I say reassuringly.

"Why would he do this?"

"John must think you are a strong woman, and you can handle this or he would be here now."

"I'm not okay," she says crying even more.

"Abbey, you have friends here, you have me, and I will stay with you until John gets back."

"No, you have to get home to your children."

"My children aren't even coming home tonight," I tell her. "I am happy to stay with you. I sleep on the couch at home. I can sleep on the couch here."

"No, I'm ok now. This is John's job. He should be here." Eventually, I leave, because I am the friend who cannot insist on staying over.

"Wait for me in the morning. I will be back to get you."

"Ok, I'll see you in the morning."

Wild Animal Noises and Other Confusions

Early the next morning, I ring the buzzer to get into her building. There's no answer.

Another resident is leaving the building, and I slide through the open door. I run up the stairs to her floor. My heart sinks. The apartment door is wide open. As I walk into the room, I see her purse, her keys, and her cell phone sitting on the dining room table.

"Abbey?" There is no answer. She is gone. I quickly run through the rooms, hoping to find her, but the rooms are empty.

I'm beginning to panic. I don't know when she left, or where she has gone. She has no identification on her and there is no way to reach her. I call John, but there is no answer.

As I run through the lobby door, I see one of the security guards and I ask him about Abbey. "I think I saw her a while ago walking down the street that way," he points.

As I head down the road, my cell phone rings. It is the woman from the administration office. "Abbey is here with me. She was looking for you."

"I'm looking for her. I will be right over." My heart is pounding as I walk toward the office.

Abbey is happy to see me. "I couldn't remember where you lived."

"I thought you were going to wait for me to come over."

"I was waiting for you, but then I heard a noise, and I went outside to look for it."

"What kind of noise?"

"Kind of like a wild animal."

I suppose there's no point in trying to ask her what she would have done if the noise really had been some wild animal. The point I need to make is with John. She cannot be left alone.

"Do you want to get some coffee?" she asks me. I look at her. She is wearing the same clothes, her sweater is on inside out, and she has two different shoes on.

"Sure. Do you have your purse?"

She checks both hands. "No."

"Ok, let's go back to the apartment to get it."

She seems exhausted. I wonder if she slept last night. Gently, I persuade her to change her sweater, and I pull out a pair of clean underpants for her. I leave the bedroom to give her some privacy. A few minutes later we are on our way to Starbucks.

We order our usual coffee drinks and some oatmeal. She wants to pay today, so we wait for her to find her credit card. The usual zipping and unzipping of the purse occurs. This is followed by the predictable, "I hate this purse. I need to get a new one."

She pulls out her grandfather's watch, some photographs and the clean pair of underwear that I handed her this morning. The girl behind the register, Abbey, and I are all equally surprised.

78

"How did that get in here?" she laughs.

"It's just one of those days," I chime in. "Hey, let me pay for coffee."

"Oh, good," she says, and stuffs the panties back into the purse.

"Today is my birthday," I tell her, as we sip our coffee. "Would you like to get a manicure and pedicure?"

"I would love to. I'll even treat you since it's your birthday."

I'm not sure if accepting this would be the right thing to do. From time to time, Abbey offers to pay for gas or something, but then she forgets about it when the time actually comes.

When we get to the salon, Abbey looks delighted. She sprawls out in the massage chair. She is beaming as two attendants fuss over her hands and feet. They show her a tray of colors and she chooses a pretty red polish. The women begin to massage her hands and feet. Abbey deflates, sinking deeply into the cushions of the oversized chair. She smiles blissfully and then closes her eyes. She is completely relaxed. A few minutes later she is snoring. The women painting her nails are giggling and trying not to disturb her. When it's over, she wakes up and tells them, "I loved this. Next time I'm getting a wild color."

She still needs a bath or a shower, but I am her friend, and she is not a child. So, I decide the next best thing will be a chlorine dunk in the swimming pool.

"Today is such a beautiful day. Would you like to go swimming in our pool?" I ask her.

"Yes, I need to get some exercise," she says.

We head back to my apartment first, so I can grab my swimsuit.

"Wow, your apartment is really messy. I like that." She walks around the rooms, nodding approvingly.

"We just moved over to this apartment last weekend. We haven't had time to unpack all the boxes yet." She seems to be inspecting the papers on my desk, and I'm hoping that I haven't left any incriminating messages around. I grab my bathing suit, "Ok, let's go to your apartment and get your swimsuit."

"Even your kitchen is messy," she is quite pleased with this discovery. I'm glad someone finds it amusing.

We get to her apartment. "Can I use this bathroom to change into my bathing suit?" I ask politely.

"Yes, I'll use John's bathroom." I throw on my suit and cover up and wait in the living room for her. A few minutes later, Abbey comes walking out completely naked, carrying her bathing suit in her hands like a small offering. "Can you help me with this?"

"Of course, these bathing suits are so tricky and hard to get on." She reminds me of a small, vulnerable child.

She balances on my shoulder as she steps into the bathing suit. I act as though walking around naked and needing help to get dressed are just normal everyday events.

80

The Secret Friend

We walk through the gates to the main pool at our apartment complex. Abbey says she is going to do some laps. I join her in the pool, and I pretend not to watch her as I do my water aerobics exercises. She swims from the shallow end of the pool to the deep end. She turns to swim back and then stops. She appears to be bobbing up and down in the water where the pool is ten feet deep. She doesn't seem to be in trouble, but I'm wondering why she is hovering in one spot.

Could Alzheimer's cause her to forget how to swim right in the middle of the pool? The rescue pole is hanging a few feet away. I look at the other people around us and try to figure out who would be most likely to help me save her if she starts to drown.

"Hey Abbey, the pool feels good today, doesn't it?" I hope that getting her attention will cause her to be more aware and it works. She waves at me and starts swimming. It's just like worrying about a small child again.

When we get home, she wants to put on something pretty, because John is coming home to take her out to dinner. She can't wait to show him her fancy nails. I help her pick out some clothes and get ready for her big date. John calls to say he is on his way, and she is very excited. We sit out on the patio and wait for John to arrive. I can see the finish line and I start to relax. I'm really proud of both of us; she has survived the separation, and I have kept her safe and happy.

Suddenly, Abbey jumps up and starts making strange birdlike noises. She is staring up into the trees. I'm watching her in disbelief. Everything was going so well. Did she just lose her connection to reality? Is she communicating with someone, or something, that's not there? I thought we were so close to success and now she has totally lost it. I'm just sitting there, not sure what to do next.

Then, I hear something whistling back. And like two courting doves, John and Abbey call to each other, whoo hoo, whoo hoo hoo. Abbey stops and looks at me, "You have to go now, but don't call me, because I'm going to be having lots of wild sex tonight."

Wow. I walk home and all I can think about is going to sleep. I remember that it is my birthday, but I'm way too tired to care. I've just worked six days in a row for a total of fifty-two hours. There does seem to be some irony that I am falling into bed exhausted and alone on my birthday while Abbey is having wild sex, but I'm too tired to contemplate anything other than the position of my pillow.

The Still Alice Surprise

I wake up Sunday morning, and surprisingly, on my one day off, I want to read Still Alice. John has asked me repeatedly if I have finished the book. I've offered to return it to him, but he really wants me to read it. I know that it is written from the perspective of a woman who has Alzheimer's. I did not realize that one of the book's themes would be about end-of-life decisions.

Once I start reading, I cannot do anything else. Alice makes a plan to kill herself before Alzheimer's devastates her mind. The author touches upon doctor assisted suicide and husband assisted suicide. I wonder why John wanted me to read the book so badly.

Shake Your Money Makers

Tuesday morning arrives, and I am still asleep when my cell phone rings.

"Hi, this is Abbey. Whatcha doing?" She sounds energetic and ready to go.

"Hi. I just woke up. What are you doing?"

"Is it a Zumba day?"

"Yes, would you like to go to Zumba?"

"Yes, I'm ready to go." I look at my clock. It's only 7 a.m. Zumba does not start until 10. From the background noises, I can tell that John has the call on speakerphone. They both sound very happy.

"I can come over around 8 or 9, what time works for you?"

There is murmuring and I hear John say loudly, "Eight o'clock is good, we will eat breakfast, and then you can go to Zumba."

As I jump out of bed, I am deciding how we will fill the two hours before Zumba. Timing is very important. Abbey gets anxious if we have to wait for something to start, so we need to pace ourselves. I think we have time for Starbucks, meeting and greeting the children and their mothers. Then, we should have time to walk around the dog park.

The Secret Friend

Our town allows residents to bring their dogs to the public baseball field for two hours every weekday morning. At least fifty people and a huge assortment of dogs will be running free inside the fenced park. Abbey loves walking around the circle, and the frenetic energy of the dogs racing around the field. The Senior Center is conveniently located across the parking lot, so we can walk to our Zumba class.

Mostly, we blend in with the doggie crowd. Occasionally, the conversation becomes awkward. Sometimes someone will ask us which dog is ours. We have to say that none of them belong to us. The next logical question is, then why are you here in the dog park, but I am becoming adept at diverting the conversation.

Sometimes Abbey will ask someone if she can have their dog. People tend to laugh kindly when they answer and offer names of breeders. Sometimes after the people have walked away, Abbey will turn to me and say, "You know, I really wanted *that* dog." And then, we move on.

Abbey is dressed and ready to go when I arrive. "We got up very early this morning," John says happily,

"Abbey is excited about going to Zumba."

"Me too! Look, Abbey, I'm wearing my scrunchie!"

Abbey laughs at my bright pink hair scrunchie. "Are you really going to wear that?" she asks me.

"I am. I think it's perfect for Zumba. Would you like to borrow a scrunchie?"

"No. I'm going to pretend I don't know you," she says giggling.

"Ok, let's go find out about Zumba."

"Wait, I need some money," Abbey looks at John.

"You have money in your purse. You're locked and loaded."

"Ok, see you tonight." Abbey is ready for today's adventure.

As I walk to the driver's side of the car, I notice that Abbey is following me instead of going to the passenger side of the car. I make a sweeping gesture and walk toward her side of the car.

"Let me get the door for you today, Madam." I think making up a whimsical game will help her find her seat without hurting her feelings. She acts like royalty and thanks me as I hold the door open for her. Then she tries to get into the car headfirst and bumps her forehead on the roof of the car.

"Ouch." She looks startled and rubs her head. I brush off the passenger seat and announce that she can now safely sit down. This time, the memory of how to get into a car comes back and she slides in easily. From now on, I think I will park my car on the other side of the street. This way I can help her into her seat first.

As I start the car, Abbey turns to me and says, "I don't want to hurt your feelings, but I don't want to get my nails done again. John said that nail polish is tacky. John is going to do my nails. That's John's job."

"Oh, ok." I'm surprised to hear her say this, since she was so happy about having her nails painted. I'm starting to think that

86

every time we spend money, John gets a new job, but I'm not going to say this out loud.

Our morning unfolds perfectly as planned, coffee, the dog park and finally it's time for Zumba. As we make our way into the center, Abbey remembers our encounter with the frisky, older men.

"I don't like the people here."

"Well, let's try the Zumba class. If we don't like it, we don't have to stay."

I'm a bit apprehensive about the dance class. According to the flyers, Zumba is a party where everyone is welcome. I hope it is more of a non-judgmental free for all, and not an audition for synchronized seniors. I'm relieved to see only four other people in the room. No one looks like a professional dancer.

The teacher puts on some energetic Latin music. Abbey starts shimmying around, glowing with happiness. The teacher calls out the moves. I'm impressed that Abbey is able to follow the instructions most of the time. But then again, I notice that everyone in the class is doing their own version of Zumba. We are shaking to Shakira and twisting to the oldies.

I've brought a couple of bottles of water to class. Between songs the teacher encourages us to take a drink. Everyone is running over and taking swigs from their water bottles, except for Abbey. I grab her water bottle, twist off the top, and run over to her and say, "Water, water."

"Thanks," she doesn't seem to mind, and I realize that this is the only way she is going to get fluids during our class. After she takes a few sips, she hands the bottle back to me. I alternate between getting water for Abbey and myself. At the end of class, everyone is glowing with the rush of endorphins and sweat. We are all congratulating one another on a great class and promising to meet again at the next class.

I want to make sure Abbey feels comfortable, so I ask the teacher, "What if I never learn to do the steps?"

The teacher gives the answer I had hoped she would. "Zumba is about feeling the music and just moving. There is no right or wrong."

Abbey looks at me and rolls her eyes, "Just try your best. Don't worry about it," she says.

The other women say goodbye. The teacher, Abbey, and I are the last ones left gathering up our belongings. Just as we are about to leave, a petite, energetic blond comes sweeping into the room. She is perfectly tailored in a proper little checked suit. Her hair is obediently straight and smooth. She looks like she is on a mission. She is accompanied by a tall stately woman dressed in a rainbow of colorful clothing and a turban. She is introduced as a visitor from a small village in Kenya.

The blond is giving her a tour of the Senior Center.

"This is our dance studio," the suit says proudly. Dance studio, otherwise known as the cafeteria, as soon as the partition is rolled back in approximately two minutes, I think to myself. The visitor smiles sweetly. Abbey is immediately entranced by this exotic woman with beautiful chocolate skin.

"You just missed our Zumba class," the teacher tells them regretfully. Both women seem disappointed. The little blond says she has never actually been to a class, but she has heard good things about Zumba. Our visitor says she loves music and dancing, but she has never heard of this Zumba dance.

"We dance to music from around the world," says our teacher, making us sound like some sort of global dance troupe.

"We can show you how to do it," Abbey says excitedly. "C'mon we'll teach you."

I look at the little blond in high heels, and she is adamantly shaking her head.

"No, no, but we would love to see you perform." Her guest politely declines the invitation to dance but says she too would like to watch.

Panic sweeps over me. Are we really are going to embarrass ourselves in front of these strangers? We've had one class and suddenly we're giving an international recital? Are we really going to perform as representatives of the dance abilities of American women?

I can almost hear the story when our visitor returns to her home in Kenya at the appalling movements that pass for dance in America. Perhaps, some evening sitting around a fire, the story of the awkward twitching and thrashing to noise will bring much laughter to a distant village. I want to apologize to Benito, or whoever invented Zumba, that we would have the nerve to desecrate his creation.

Abbey and the teacher are staring at me. Abbey looks excited to do this. I appear to be the final vote. "Yes, we would love to show you how to do it." I hear myself say obligingly. Clearly, Abbey's happiness is more important than sullying the image of American women in front of the rest of the world.

We do not disappoint. Our teacher puts on a rap song by an "artist" named Pit Bull, who is declaring his love for women with big booties and making "boom boom" all night long in his "crib." The three of us gyrate and flail, none of us are in sync, and the song seems to go on forever. This, I tell myself, is the day the music really died.

Abbey is putting on her best getting funky face and pulling out some old martial arts stances. The teacher looks like she is in pain. Me, I'm just terrible. I saw myself once in the mirror as I was exercising. The image was frightening. I realized that my lip curls uncontrollably just like an aging punk rocker when I'm exercising. I have avoided mirrors since then, but I have no reason to believe I look any less hideous.

Suddenly, I am grateful for the cultural proprieties that prevent us from laughing in polite situations. As I consider our odd performance, I'm not sure I could show the same restraint. In the end, the lovely ladies are thanking us, Abbey is beaming with delight, and I know that sacrificing a little ego is a good thing.

Chapter 4 March

What's a Boundary, or Where do You End and I Begin?

Our routine has expanded again. Abbey and I are spending five or six days a week together. The total hours per week range from forty to fifty-five. Our starting time varies; some days are as early as 7 a.m., or as late as 10 a.m. Abbey will call me every morning and ask me if I have any time for her, or if it is a Zumba day.

Sometimes, John will send me a text message telling me that Abbey is about to call me. Some days, I am waiting for the phone call, wondering if this system really makes sense. Our day together ends eight, nine, or more hours later, depending on when John returns from work. Usually, John will call when he is close to home and Abbey can expect him within 15 or 20 minutes. John believes it is safe to leave Abbey alone for this short amount of time.

Each night, I come home and send an email to John describing our daily adventures. Then, I design the next day's activities. I look through the "what's going on" section of our local online newspapers. I have subscribed to numerous event notifications. Our local colleges post talks with interesting people, exhibitions, and odd gatherings. I watch for special events at public places, parks, gardens, and street fairs. I keep our outings within a one hour driving radius. Each day looks like a spontaneous dance, but I have carefully choreographed the moves ahead of time.

Since I am not aware of any formal guidelines for a Secret Friend, I create my own job description.

I suggest activities based on Abbey's interests and abilities. I incorporate exercise, healthy food choices, socialization, novel experiences, activities that will trigger memories, and fun. Each day is an adventure, full of possibilities, presents just waiting to be unwrapped, mystery and surprise.

I keep us engaged, learning, laughing, singing and dancing. We are an enrichment program, field trip specialists, explorers, and fun seekers. We tumble along collecting friends, good times, and silly stories. It is my secret hope that we will find a miracle and Abbey will live happily ever after and remember it all.

When I tell this to John, he sends me another ambiguous compliment.

"Yes, you have stimulated her social interests. She is no longer willing to sit in apartment and do nothing. She wants me to go to places that you have taken her."

Each day starts the same way. "Would you like to get some coffee?"

It is our simple ritual that opens the door to infinite possibilities. The only other constant is Zumba, which meets twice a week. I know we will need to eat lunch and coordinate with John's return home. The rest of the day is a blank canvas, colored only by keeping Abbey interested and happy.

The Secret Friend

One morning I walk into John and Abbey's apartment, and I can smell the coffee brewing.

"Hey, why don't you and Abbey have coffee here today?" John says pointing to the kitchen.

"Um, no, thank you," I say hesitatingly.

"We like to go to Starbucks," Abbey tells him.

"But it's expensive to go there every day," John says.

This is part of our ritual. John and I have discussed why I use it to start the day. He's frowning as we head out the door. Before we started this arrangement, John complained that Abbey would cry and fuss when he left for work. Now, Abbey is skipping happily out the door, and he can start most of his days without drama. I think we have accomplished what he wanted. Why is he rocking the boat?

As we click our seatbelts, Abbey says, "You used to be rich, didn't you?"

"Ha, I suppose, I might have been, at one time," I say.

"But you're not rich now, are you?"

"No."

"What happened?"

"Someone stole my stock. I had over half a million shares."

"That's terrible."

"A lawyer is trying to help me get it back, but I'm not optimistic about it."

"Someone is stealing my stuff too. I hate it when people do that."

"Me, too. I hope we both get our stuff back."

"Yeah."

The Surprise Behind Door Number 2

The Senior Center has become one of our valuable resources. Boston has Cheer's, the bar where everyone knows your name. We have the Senior Center, where we are treated like celebrities when we walk into the community center.

"Here come the Zumba ladies! Good morning!" Abbey looks especially cute in her spandex outfit and the receptionists compliment her colorful choices. Wendy, the Activities Director, is happy to see us.

The Senior Center was originally created for the senior population, but they are trying to expand their reach. Zumba was introduced to pull younger members of the community into the facility. The timing is excellent for us.

On the bulletin board, I notice an announcement for a gem show. The ladies behind the desk tell us that the Senior Center has its own rock polishing studio. They direct us to an unmarked door across the hall from our Zumba room. We are surprised to discover a shop filled with wood, rocks, and dangerous looking machines. The teacher introduces himself as Preston. He is also the president of the local gem society.

Abbey tells him about her gold panning relatives and how she would like to make some jewelry. Preston is gentle and patient with us. He takes us into the back room. I watch people pressing rocks against spinning blades. This activity is not going to work for someone who sometimes forgets that she is holding a coffee cup, I tell myself. Preston says we are welcome to join his class. Abbey says she will sign up for the next one.

His organization is also sponsoring a gem show and he gives us free tickets to attend. He wants us to come back and tell him what we think of the show.

I don't know if anyone at the Senior Center realizes that Abbey has Alzheimer's. As we walk down the hall, the program director calls to us. Wendy tells us how happy she is that we are coming to the Senior Center.

Abbey tries to answer her and stumbles over her words.

"I have Alzheimer's disease," she tells Wendy.

Wendy looks surprised. "I never would have known. But I think you are very brave. And by coming here, you are teaching people about living with a disease."

"Yes, I can do everything anyone else can do," Abbey tells her proudly.

Wendy gives Abbey a hug, "thank you for telling me and I hope you keep coming to Zumba."

Abbey is glowing from Wendy's compliments. Perhaps emboldened by her disclosure, I point to a magazine on our way out of the Senior Center.

"Abbey, look, there's a story about memory." Abbey scrunches up her face and looks at me like I am crazy.

"I don't need that. I have Alzheimer's, but there's nothing wrong with my memory."

96

The Secret Friend

Hits and Misses

Some of our expeditions are more successful than others. One day we drive out to a charming town, Half Moon Bay, with a spectacular access to the Pacific Ocean. The sun is shining, the waves are crashing on the shore, surfers are running down the beach, and we are walking barefoot on the sand in the midst of it all. I imagine that Abbey will embrace this paradise. Instead, she looks bored. She picks up a couple of shells but looks like she would rather be somewhere else. I suggest a visit to a studio that I noticed on our way to the beach. Abbey perks up,

"I went there before with my father to pick out some pots. Let's go."

We pull into the parking lot and Abbey almost jumps out of the car before it has stopped.

"This is the place we used to go. I've been looking for this," she says excitedly. Statues, water fountains, and patio furniture collide with pots and plants in a colorful kaleidoscope.

Abbey darts toward the brightest colored pots, "I saw these in Mexico." The tag says hand painted in Mexico. We move through rooms of pottery and glasswork. Abbey has the enthusiasm of a small child on Christmas morning. "Look at this glaze. I like this shape."

Then, we discover the most amazing treasure of all. In back of the building, there must be over two hundred pots of all sizes, shapes, and colors spread out over a huge space. Abbey wants me to take her picture with all the pots. I've brought a couple of the

98

new disposable cameras. She poses next to her favorite pieces of art, and I snap away as she grins. After a couple of hours, she makes her final decision and chooses a plant and a pot that we can fit into the car.

We head back over the mountain, victorious, with Abbey holding the plant in her lap. I offer to place it in the back seat, but she insists on holding it. I wonder if she is afraid of forgetting it. She is also hungry and wants to go back to that same place to eat.

"Bucks?" I guess.

"Yes, I like it there." Bucks Restaurant is in the very well to do town of Woodside. There was a time when I would have cared about how we looked before sitting down among the rich and famous, but I am over it now.

Bucks looks especially busy, and I take the only available parking spot, directly in front of the large restaurant windows. My car is over ten years old and looks out of place among the brand new, fancy models around us. The remote control for my car is broken, so getting out of the car is a bit tricky. I have to open my door and get out. Then, Abbey will copy me. I can no longer lock my car with the remote without setting off the alarm system. Once Abbey is out of the car, I can lock the doors manually.

In a slow-motion nightmarish scenario, I see Abbey hit the lock button just as my car door is closing. I grab it to stop it from closing, but it is too late. The alarm system is triggered, the headlights are flashing, and the horn is blasting. Abbey has locked herself in the car. I'm frantically pressing the remote button trying to shut off the security system. Abbey has her hands over her ears. Everyone is watching us. The flashing headlights are illuminating the diners sitting by the windows. Disgruntled faces glare at us as the lights flash and the horn blares.

A tall, perfected coiffed woman runs over and grabs the keys out of my hands.

"Really? Do I look stupid?" I think to myself.

After a few tries, she hands the keys back to me. "It's not working."

I open the car door with the key.

"I'm so sorry, Abbey. I think we need to drive to the car dealership."

"I'm just going to walk home," she tells me.

"No, no, we are really close to the shop, and they can fix it." I start the car quickly and we drive away flashing and honking. No one tries to stop us.

After the cacophony subsides, I pull over and send John a text message. We agree to meet in a parking lot on the grounds of our apartment complex. John pulls in right behind me. I warn Abbey that the noise will start again when we open the car doors. The unsettling noise and light show resumes. John comes over and tells me to release the hood on my car. After a bit of tinkering, he disengages the security system, and the ear deafening horn is silenced.

As we are standing there appreciating the silence, a runner passes by and says hello to us. We all return the greeting.

John turns to Abbey, "Do you know who that was?"

He doesn't look like anyone I recognize, and Abbey doesn't seem to have any clue either. Abbey and I both shake our heads no.

"That's your doctor. Your Alzheimer's doctor," John says, a little bit smugly, I think.

"Oh, him. I hate him. He doesn't do anything for me," Abbey says dismissively.

Gold Rush Glitter Girls

The day of the gem show arrives, and Abbey is excited about hunting for gold treasures. The Conference Center is packed with aisles of vendors who have traveled from all over the United States to show off their jewelry. Under the bright lights, beads and jewels glitter and beckon. The sellers are as colorful as their creations.

Abbey asks a lot of questions and repeats her story about her relative who was taken from an Indian reservation by someone to pan for gold in California. Some of the details have changed, but the overall story remains. The vendors think Abbey is adorable.

As we move through the hall, I notice that Abbey is holding a necklace. She has not bought anything, and I realize she must have accidentally walked away with it. I have no idea where she picked it up, and I'm sure she didn't mean to steal it. I'm not going to make a big deal over it or embarrass her. I will just have to watch her more closely.

We both see the table of scrunchies at the same time.

"Abbey, look, it's my favorite thing, scrunchies!"

She starts laughing, "Don't embarrass me."

"Come over here. I'll buy you a scrunchie."

She is inching away and giggling, "I would never wear a scrunchie."

"They are three for ten dollars and I can wear them to Zumba."

The Secret Friend

Scrunchies make Abbey laugh, so I choose three outrageous pink, green, and blue ones. Some have shiny baubles on them, and I tell Abbey I cannot go home without them. She is shaking her head and smiling as she tells the scrunchie seller that I am crazy.

After the show, we go to a buffet style restaurant with endless salad ingredients, and reasonable prices.

Abbey walks right past the setup table, so I grab a tray and two plates. She stands beside me as I read the signs out loud and she tells me what she wants on her plate. She can still make choices, but the physical maneuvering is becoming too complex.

At the register, I ask for help in getting our food to the table. When the cashier asks about drinks, Abbey says she wants a beer. She wants to hear the selections, and then chooses one. She can still pick a beer out of a lineup. I make a note to ask John how he handles this situation. We talk about the gem show as we enjoy our healthy meal. It's been a good day.

Missed Connections

As we leave the restaurant my cell phone rings.

"Abbey, it's my daughter, Katie, calling from Berkeley."

"I went to Berkeley," Abbey remembers.

"Hi, honey, Abbey and I just finished eating. What's going on?"

My daughter is excited, "I just saw Bill Clinton!"

"Abbey, Katie just saw Bill Clinton," I say.

Abbey looks around, "Where?"

"Oh, not here. In Berkeley, where she goes to school."

"Mom, are you listening to me?"

"Of course, I am. Did you talk to Bill Clinton?"

Abbey is still looking around, "I still don't see him."

"No, he drove by in a car. I think he must have given a talk here today," Katie says.

As we are walking along, I notice a man up ahead who is singing "Take me out to the ball game." He is standing on the corner, and he looks like he is either drunk, or crazy. Abbey sees him too and starts walking toward him. She starts singing the song along with him.

"Katie, I need to go."

"Don't you want to hear what happened?"

"I do, but you need to call me later." The inebriated man is smiling and swerving his way toward us.

"Mom, this won't take long."

"Katie, Abbey is about to walk away singing with a homeless guy on the corner. I have to hang up, now!" I shut the phone off and run up to avoid a potential disaster. I compliment the man on his voice and then gently guide Abbey away while we are still singing the song.

As we get back into the car, Abbey's cell phone rings. "It must be John!" We scramble to find it and answer before he hangs up. But today, it turns out to be a dear friend from the East Coast, who is calling to say hello. Abbey is turning the phone around and holding it upside down before I suggest we just put the call on speaker phone. Finally, her friend's voice is clear. Abbey tells her how much she misses her and asks about her children and her dog. While her friend is answering, Abbey remembers "the stuff" and interrupts her mid-sentence.

"Do you know where my stuff is? I think John is stealing my stuff and he won't give it to me."

A sweet voice responds, "Abbey, if I knew where your stuff was, I would put it on my back and carry it across the country for you."

"Ok. Thank you." Abbey hands the phone to me. I pick up the conversation, but Abbey appears not to be listening any longer. Her friend says that she will call John to see if she can help locate Abbey's stuff. We say our goodbyes. I realize that Abbey has just recruited another person to find her stuff.

More Surprises

That night, I get another email from Abbey's sister, Linda. I have been including her in my daily descriptions of our activities. She is coming to visit Abbey and John. She is effusive in her praise again and thanks me for including her in my daily reports.

Surprisingly, she tells me, "The Secret Friend was my idea. I jumped for joy when John found you and hearing what a giant boon you have been to Abbey's life. I am a planner, much like you, I suspect. At least six years ago, I confronted John with my heart-breaking suspicions. Years went by before a formal diagnosis was made. It's been difficult for all of us, but your existence proves that I have made some progress.

"As to your question about money and Abbey's claim that John is mad. John is very careful with money. The real Abbey was too. Spending money is new to her. Abbey inherited money from both our parents. However, this money has to last her lifetime. I look at this with two minds—first, let her have fun with it while she can, at least, appreciate it. Second, the prudent thing is to save and conserve. Sadly, I don't believe that Abbey will live long. For John and me, she is dying in increments, which is dreadful. I say— spend."

I am constantly amazed and impressed with John's love for my sister. Neither her appearance, nor her public behaviors embarrass him at all. He doesn't see other people's reaction to her, the way she looks or acts.

Abbey has threatened to divorce John for, at least, twenty-five years. Yet, I would call their marriage a successful one.

It is just her way to blow off stream.

I'm looking forward to having lunch with you and Abbey."

These new revelations amaze me. "I'm really looking forward to lunch, too. Let me know when you get here," I write back.

Just before Linda's arrival, I receive a text message from John. "I think Abbey needs to spend time alone with her sister. Maybe you can join them next time."

I'm disappointed, but I'm willing to abide by his wishes. Linda shows up on time and throws her arms around Abbey.

"How are you, kiddo? I love your colorful top," Linda says.

"I just got it. John was mad about it," Abbey says.

Linda looks stern, "You tell him, you have money, and you can buy anything you want."

Linda is tall and elegant, with beautiful silver hair. But I also think she would wrestle a bear to the ground to protect her own cubs. She seems very protective of Abbey.

"Will you help me get my stuff?" Abbey asks her sister.

"John said there's some stuff in storage," I say trying to clarify the "stuff" issue.

Linda says she will talk to John. Abbey may have Alzheimer's, but she still knows how to recruit a team to accomplish her goals.

I try to gracefully excuse myself from the lunch plans. Abbey seems very happy to be with her sister. I think maybe John's assessment was correct.

Later, I send Linda an email, "I hope your visit went well. John told me not to join you for lunch, so you and Abbey could enjoy some sisterly time together. Maybe we can have lunch another time."

"Regarding lunch—we received opposite instructions from John. I want you to know how happy you make the three of us— John, Abbey, and me. Thank you."

Homecoming

At the end of March, John says that they will move to a much bigger apartment and Abbey's stuff will be delivered. Abbey is ecstatic with this news. She can remember some of the items that belonged to her father and other family members, but she is anxious to see what has been in storage.

The new apartment building is at the other end of the complex. Her new apartment will look more like a home. She will not have to use an elevator, and she will have a huge patio area. When we go to look at it, Abbey asks me if she will own this home. I tell her I am not sure. A lovely courtyard and swimming pool are located directly behind the new apartment. Abbey asks me if this is her yard. I am torn between wanting her to be happy and telling her the truth. I say I think it must be hers, unless someone says that it is not.

I try to help orient her to the new location. We walk to the rental office, to the tennis courts and back to her new apartment.

"You are moving uptown to the fancy part of town," I tell Abbey.

"Yeah, I like the new place."

I show her how the new place is facing the creek just like her old place. We stand on the path next to the creek and I tell her that this is the same street where she lives now. But each time she looks down the street, she asks me the same question, "What's down there?"

The Secret Friend

So, we walk along the creek from the old apartment to the new apartment and back again. Despite the creek and the walk, she still seems confused. Finally, she tells me it doesn't matter. "Sometimes it's good to have Alzheimer's," she says, "People do a lot of things for you. The security guards will bring me home."

Holi Holi Holi

Moving day finally arrives with a flurry of text messages from John. "Difficult situation. Do you have any time to take her out?"

The packing is not going well. The apartment is covered with moving cartons that are being emptied as fast as they are being filled. John is wrapping and packing their worldly goods for the transition to the new living space.

Abbey has the look of a young child at a birthday party; wide eyed and eager to unwrap the mysteries of each package. Each time she pulls an item out of the box, she is happily surprised, as if seeing the object for the first time. Then, she moves on to the next box.

John gives up on an organized system of packing. He starts shoving their stuff into boxes and sealing them before she has a chance to take them apart.

She pulls something heavy out of a box and starts to unwrap it.

"We're moving. We need to pack, just leave the stuff alone," he says. Frustration is creeping into his voice.

"Don't tell me what to do," she says, "I don't want to move." She is getting angry.

"We are moving to a bigger apartment. You liked it when you saw it." The aggravation is obvious.

The Secret Friend

"I want a house with a garden. And I want a dog." She is clinging to the newspaper wrapper when something drops out of her hands and smashes onto the floor. She looks devastated. "That belonged to my mother."

"No, it didn't."

"Well, I want a divorce."

"Hello!" I say. I walk through the open door into the raging tornado. "I heard some music playing across the street. Anyone want to go with me?"

John looks exhausted and frustrated. "Abbey would like to go."

She is happy to see me. "I want a new husband," she says, not caring that the current one is standing right next to her. "I should have married Juan Carlos. He was from Brazil."

I smile, it amazes me that she cannot remember her current address or phone number, but she can remember the name of her high school crush from over 40 years ago.

"Abbey, would you like to go get some coffee? We can find out where the music is coming from." I'm hoping that I can convince her to leave the apartment, and it seems to work.

"Yes. I'm ready." She walks out the door and doesn't look back.

John looks relieved and says, "Have fun and don't hurry back."

Abbey and I cross the street and head toward the sound of laughter and music coming from one of the fields. As we get closer, we see a strange gathering of men, women, and children throwing handfuls of colored powder at each other. Abbey walks right up to the fence separating the colorful people and us. Swirls of color float through the air and people are laughing as their hair, faces, and bodies disappear under the rainbow of color.

"I want to do that" she tells me.

"Let's find out what this is all about," I say. I've already researched the event, but I'm assessing the safety factors. I'm a little concerned about the size of the crowd, although the group does seem to be fenced in.

A couple of people standing on the other side of the divider overhear our conversation. "Do you want to join us?" they ask gleefully. "We're celebrating Holi, the Indian festival for the New Year! Everyone throws colored powder on each other and then we all dance."

Abbey sticks her face over the fence, "I want some color!" I wonder if the powder will stain our clothes, but she is through the gate and people are rubbing red, green, and yellow dye on her face and in her hair. She is beaming with joy.

"Happy Holi!" people are shouting. There must be over two hundred people prancing around the field, a rainbow of painted faces giggling and rubbing color onto strangers.

"C'mon. Let's get some color," Abbey says. She is totally enthralled with this activity. Someone directs us to the huge sacks

114

of powder. She takes a big handful of pink color and gleefully rubs it into my hair.

"I've always wanted pink hair," I say, "How did you know?" She is grinning at me. I have never seen her happier than at this moment.

We both grab handfuls of the colored powder and toss them at each other. We are children again, laughing and carefree. We are the painters and the canvas. Other people run up behind us and sprinkle us with color.

We squeal with delight and then rub colored powder into their hair and all over their clothes. She is overjoyed with this event and soon we blend into the crowd dancing and singing. We drift toward the musicians on stage, and she is bumping her hips and rubbing shoulders with everyone around her.

Suddenly, some children come running through the crowd with squirt guns, spraying us all with water. The colors run together, and we are all screaming, "Happy Holi!" We are united as one body, everyone equal, transcending time, trouble, and disease. We are in a place of total acceptance and joy, celebrating the possibilities of the year to come. The sun is shining, we are in the moment, nothing else matters.

"Happy Holi! Holi, Holi, Holi!" In the midst of this crazy crowd, outdoors in a field, hand painted by strangers, we have discovered a place where Alzheimer's cannot find us. A few hours later, the music ends, and we spill back out into the world.

She turns to me, "I want to do this again."

"Ok, we will!"

I take another look at us. We are almost unrecognizable drenched in colors, our hair is wet, our clothes have taken on new identities and the powder seems to have seeped into every pore and crevice in our skin.

As we walk back home, people are smiling and pointing at us. Abbey is sauntering along, enjoying the attention. I remember her husband's words about helping her feel "normal." I'm not sure this falls into the "normal" category, but personally, I'll take happy over normal any day!

Emergency Wake Up Call

When I get home, I add up the time I have spent with Abbey for the past week. I'm not surprised to see that I have just worked 53 hours. I've probably spent another ten hours on the computer planning our days. My clothes are soggy, and my hair is pink. I need to shower, get some sleep, and get ready for Zumba in the morning. I don't remember falling into bed.

Sometime around 3 a.m., I wake up and realize that I cannot move. The pain in my chest is sharp, and my body refuses to budge. No one else is home. I think I may be having a heart attack. I concentrate on my breathing and eventually I am able to reach my cell phone. I dial a friend who lives in my apartment complex. The answering machine comes on and I leave a rather panicky message.

Slowly, I get myself up and pull on a little sundress. I walk carefully down to my car and manage the drive to the Stanford Emergency Room. The guard allows me to park by the entrance and I make my way through security to the receptionist. It's almost 4 a.m. and the waiting room is empty. When I mention my chest pain, a doctor appears quickly. They hook me up to some machines and ask a million questions. I am still in pain, but my breathing has improved. One of the cute, young doctors asks me if anyone has given me the lecture about driving myself to the ER.

"I live very close. I can almost see the ER from my apartment on Sand Hill Road. I did make one phone call, but you can give me the lecture, if you need to." I can't help smiling, as I listen to this person, who is young enough to be my son, give me the "talk."

"Is there any one you want to contact?" he asks.

"Only if you find a problem," I say, "Otherwise, I'm not going to bother anyone."

I wait until 6 a.m. to send a text message to John. "Sorry, I cannot come over today. I'm in the ER. I will call you later."

My cell phone rings almost immediately. "What's wrong?" John sounds wide awake.

I tell him about the pain and the tests. "John, I'm sorry, I'm not going to be able to go to Zumba today."

The doctor walks into my room and says sarcastically, "I just hate it when I have to miss Zumba because I might have had a heart attack." He gives me a look of incredulity. "Time to get off the phone and take care of yourself."

I hang up the phone and try to explain. "This is my job."

He doesn't flinch. "Sounds like you need a new job. Now, stay off the phone and relax."

The first test results come back negative. My doctor returns, he is moving me to another room. I ask if more tests are really necessary. He gives me another look and says, yes.

After I am settled into the new bed, the cardiologist comes in to talk with me. She asks me about my diet, exercise, and stress. I tell her about my job as a secret friend. As I am explaining the

118

complexities, I notice someone else entering my room. I am startled to see Abbey and John come through the door.

"How did you get in here?" I ask them.

"We told them we were family," John says beaming at me.

Abbey comes over and rubs the top of my head. "Are you ok?"

"Yes, I think so," I say, "The doctor was just talking to me."

"How is she, doctor?" John asks.

"Well, I think she can go home today."

"Oh, good," Abbey says. "You know, you kind of ruined my day. I wanted to go to Zumba with you." Her honesty makes me laugh.

"Abbey, we need to hear what the doctor has to say," John chimes in. We all look at the doctor.

"I think Susan can go home, but she should probably take it easy for today."

"Is it okay for her to drive?" John asks the doctor.

It's weird to hear people talking about me, when I'm right here.

"Do you need a ride?" John asks me.

"No, I'm parked right outside the door. I drove myself over."

"You can always call us" John says.

"Thanks," I say, "I will call you when I feel better."

Abbey rubs my head again, "I was worried about you."

"I'll be fine. We will be back at Zumba soon."

"Ok, I'll call you."

I watch them leave the room and I realize how stressful this situation has become. I know we have to set up some boundaries. Two days later, Zumba trumps balance.

Chapter 5 April

Putting the Pieces Together

Wendy has invited us to a group birthday party at the Senior Center for anyone celebrating a birthday in April. She promises us cake, and music by our friend, Felton, and we readily agree.

Felton is a self-taught musician from New Orleans. He gives guitar lessons at the Senior House. Some days, he is sitting alone, and he gives us a private performance while he is waiting for a client to show up. He is one of our favorite new friends.

When we arrive, the long portable kitchen tables have been set up in front of the elevated stage. Everyone in the room has white hair. A few of the guests appear to have already fallen asleep. Our friend, Felton, is adjusting the microphone for his guitar.

"Hi Felton!" Abbey is thrilled to see our buddy.

Felton waves back, "Hi Abbey! Welcome to the party!"

We sit down and listen to Felton's gravelly voice sing one of Abbey's favorite songs, "Mustang Sally."

Wendy encourages everyone to get up and dance, but the audience is as stiff as statues.

Abbey looks at me, "Is it ok to get up?"

"Sure, do you want to dance?"

"Yes, I'm going to show them how to do it."

"Ok, go for it."

Abbey marches up the stairs and joins Felton on stage. She is wearing her long, denim skirt and she starts swirling it like she's dancing the cancan. The audience has perked up and some people even start to clap. Sensing the encouragement from the crowd, Abbey becomes even more animated, and the skirt is climbing higher.

Suddenly, I'm worried. What if she is not wearing underwear today? I hope she is not going to flash the oldies. Then again, maybe it would put a smile on their faces. The song ends and Abbey saunters over and kisses Felton on the top of his brown head. The crowd claps wildly. Abbey takes a little bow and comes back to our table.

As she takes her seat, she says to me "There, I showed them how to do it."

As we are leaving the Senior Center we pass the community bulletin board. I notice a flyer offering free tickets to a seminar on aging at Stanford University. The all-day event is being sponsored by the Senior Games. We circle back to find our friend, Wendy.

"We would love to go," I tell Wendy.

"Well, I would love to give you both free tickets," she says, "There are talks, a short movie, and a free lunch."

"Oh yeah, we'll be there," Abbey confirms.

122

The Secret Friend

Wendy gives us a schedule of events, "It's being held on campus. I will see you both there."

I imagine that Abbey will not be interested in spending a full day in lectures, but I see that 23andMe is giving a talk right after lunch. 23andMe is a company researching DNA and the links to disease and wellness. I think Abbey might like to hear the speaker. This event is followed by a short film about an aging athlete, a few words by the film maker, and a closing reception. Enrichment, socialization, and novelty are some of the ingredients I look for when designing a day. The free food is a bonus.

We arrive in time to pick up our brown bag lunch and eat outdoors at the picnic tables. A few people join us at our table. We enjoy our free lunch and conversation with new people. Abbey recognizes Wendy and we thank her again for the free tickets.

Lunch ends and we take our seats inside the small lecture hall along with about one hundred people. A professor introduces the representative from 23andMe. He talks about the research, their mission, and shows us some slides about their company. He explains how identifying DNA markers will lead to better diagnosis and prediction of disease, and hopefully cures. He mentions Alzheimer's and a couple of other diseases.

"Why do you suppose we are not further along in discovering more cures for diseases?" he asks the group.

"Money!" Abbey shouts out across the otherwise silent room.

The speaker asks, "Who said that?"

Abbey answers confidently, "I did."

"Well, you are absolutely correct! Money. We need more money to make more progress," he says.

Abbey gives me a proud smile and says to me knowingly, "It's always about money."

We are sitting in a room filled with professors, researchers, and experts, and I am thrilled for so many reasons. Abbey has been able to follow the conversation, recognize the question, had the courage to speak up, and answered the question correctly. I wish that everyone in the room could understand the significance of the moment. I see Wendy smiling at us and I am struggling to keep the tears from falling.

After the talk, we move over to the next building with the crowd. I recognize a couple of people, and we say hello. We have just settled into our seats, when Abbey says to me, "I know that woman. I went to school with her kids." The woman is standing at the podium, and I wonder if Abbey really knows her. I check our program, and it turns out the woman is from our town and is the creator of the film.

"Her name is Dorothy," I tell Abbey.

"I know. She lived next door to us when we were growing up."

The film holds Abbey's attention and Dorothy is a fascinating speaker. At the end of the event, we spill out into the sunlight and Abbey turns to me and says, "That was fun. I'm so glad you're not one of those women who just sits at home all day."

The Secret Friend

Breaking Bread

John sends me an email. His parents are coming to town for a couple of days. Unfortunately, he has to work on the first day. He asks me if I will take Abbey and his parents out to lunch and maybe show them around town. From his email, it sounds as though they are advanced in age and limited in mobility. I think they might enjoy lunch at our local seafood restaurant and a trip to the shoreline. I bring some bread to feed the ducks.

Abbey introduces me to John's father and mother. They look healthy to me. We enjoy our meal, although I notice that his mom is rather quiet. Abbey is excited to take them to Shoreline Park.

As Abbey talks to them, I drive to the duck pond. I pull the car into our favorite spot and notice a new sign. It is no longer legal to feed the birds. Who makes these rules? We have built up expectations, I have the bread, and the birds look like they were expecting us. A mother and father and two small children start throwing bread to the ducks. I call out to them.

"We wanted to feed the birds, but there's a new sign today that says it's illegal. Did you see it?" I say.

The father laughs, "You know how it is; yesterday it was legal, today it's illegal, and tomorrow it will be legal again."

"People have been feeding birds forever. I don't see how a little bread is going to make them domesticated," I say in frustration.

The Secret Friend

Suddenly, the birds are going crazy, squawking, and flapping their wings. A red fox comes running out through the mass of birds. We all scream, and he veers back into the underbrush without even scoring a feather.

Even if feeding the birds encourages them to become a bit more complacent, the fox is going to keep them on their toes or wingtips.

At this point, neither of John's parents want to get out of the car. So, driving through the parking lot is going to be the closest we are going to get to wildlife. I drive through the adjacent lot so they can get a better view of the bay.

As our wheels crunch over the gravel, a Ring-necked pheasant comes running up to our vehicle. What are the chances we would see the birds, a fox, and this unusual pheasant all in one day without even getting out of the car?

"Stop the car," Abbey says, "I want to feed the bird."

"We do too, we do too," John's parents chirp.

They all start throwing bread out the window of the car. The pheasant runs over, picks up the bread, and runs back into the tall grass. As soon as I move the car over the crushed stones, the pheasant runs back out and grabs another piece of bread. Abbey and the parents are howling with delight. From their reaction, this could be a new Disneyland attraction.

Bread is being thrown everywhere, only about half of it is making it out the car window. I wonder if the "Do Not Feed the Ducks" sign applies to this bird. We are directly in front of the park ranger's house. I think he would put a stop to this if it really mattered. I toss my bread into the wind.

After we have laughed ourselves silly, I'm not sure I can think of anything that will top this. John's parents have flown several thousand miles. I'm mentally running through our local sightseeing options when John's dad says he would like to see Nordstrom's Department Store. He was a salesman and has always wanted to visit the store.

As the four of us are walking through the handbags section, I'm considering the distribution of responsibility. John's dad is watching his wife, I'm watching Abbey, but I'm also responsible for returning the group home safely. We are browsing through women's sportswear, when John's dad says he wants to go look at men's shoes.

"We can all go together," I say.

"Mom's tired," he says, "Just stay right here. I'll be right back," and he walks away.

Almost immediately, the mom doesn't feel well. She wants to go to the car.

"Look here's some chairs. Do you want to sit down? We can just wait here," I say. She sinks into one of the seats.

"I'll take her to the car," Abbey says. I'm sure Abbey has no idea where the car is located. But that small detail is lost in the desire to be helpful and kind.

The mom gets up from the chair, "Thank you, Abbey."

128

Obviously, staying with them is a better scenario then losing both of them. "Sure, we can call your husband on his cell phone."

"He doesn't have a cell phone," the mom says.

"Really? Who doesn't have a cell phone?" I think to myself. We walk to the car. The mom slides into the back seat, leans her head back against the cushion and closes her eyes. Abbey and I are standing outside the car.

I'm wondering how we are ever going to find the dad.

Abbey volunteers. "I'll go in and find dad."

I do a quick assessment. As far as I'm concerned, I've already lost John's dad, John's mother seems to have passed out in the car, and Abbey is about to wander away. I'm a few seconds away from dialing 911, when the dad comes strolling out of the store.

"Dad! Over here! I found him!" Abbey seems to be taking the credit for finding him.

I explain quickly. "We had to come back to the car. Your wife didn't feel well. Will you take a look at her?"

The dad shakes her arm, and she mumbles something. "She's fine. She does this all the time."

I think it's time to go home.

Searching for Long Lost Relatives

Later that week, we are signed up to attend a lady's luncheon in the clubhouse at our apartment complex. For five dollars each, we will enjoy lunch, conversation with our neighbors, and a movie.

Abbey sits across the table from me talking with our good friend, Margret. I am close enough to intervene if there's a problem, but I think it's also good for her to talk with someone other than me. Abbey tells one of the women that she looks like one of her stepmothers, Stephanie. The woman lived at our complex at one time, and I ask if anyone knew her.

One of the women says to me, "You know Stephanie. She was in our water aerobics class."

"That Stephanie? That's Abbey's stepmother?" I am shocked to realize that I know Abbey's stepmother.

"Where does she live now?"

"She moved to another facility about half an hour away," one of the ladies says.

"Abbey," I say, "I know Stephanie, and I know where she lives."

"Let's go see her now," Abbey says, "I've been looking for her."

"Ok, let's finish lunch and then we'll go and visit her."

Abbey eats faster than I have ever seen her eat, and then asks me, "Can we go see Stephanie now?"

"Sure, let's drive down to her complex and see if she is home."

Stephanie is famous for traveling all over the world. "What are the chances she would be home?" I ask myself.

Abbey is excited at the possibility of seeing her and I assume the feeling will be mutual.

About an hour later, we drive up to a huge complex with massive grounds. The facility is bright and airy, and I think I wouldn't mind living there. Abbey tells the receptionist that she wants to see her stepmother and asks for her by name. A phone call is made, and we are told that Stephanie is on her way down to see us.

Stephanie is tall, thin, and appears to have more energy than most people I know, even though she is in her upper eighties. She looks happy to see us as she bounces across the lobby.

Abbey jumps up to greet her, and I'm thinking how odd it is that I already know Abbey's stepmother.

"I'm sorry, to just drop in on you," I say, "But I just found out at the ladies' luncheon that you and Abbey are related. We didn't know if you would be here, but Abbey really wanted to see you."

Stephanie is elegant and gracious. "I'm so happy to see you. Come upstairs and I'll show you my apartment. Abbey, how are you?"

"I'm fine. Did you know that my father died?"

"Yes, I was there," she says, "I was holding his hand." I am surprised to hear this, since there had been another wife after Stephanie.

"It was very sad." Abbey adds.

Stephanie looks at her, "You know, he didn't have Alzheimer's. He had a brain tumor that made it seem like he had Alzheimer's."

Abbey doesn't answer. I wonder if this means there's a chance that Abbey does not have Alzheimer's either.

Stephanie shows Abbey some paintings and furniture that had belonged to Abbey's dad. Abbey asks about some houses they used to own and some kids who actually came with another wife. Stephanie is very sweet and answers Abbey's questions patiently.

"How lovely this visit has been," I think. The serendipity of the universe has brought us all together. Stephanie's phone rings. Her friends are waiting to go to dinner with her. We take our leave and promise to keep in touch. Abbey seems happy to have finally gotten to see her stepmother again.

The next time I see our neighbor, I thank her for telling us where to find Stephanie.

"Oh," she says, "I spoke with Stephanie. I hope you weren't thinking of going back to see her. She said Abbey was an awful woman and she really doesn't want you to bring her back."

132

Who's Who and Who Cares?

These versions of Abbey are baffling to me. I consider the Abbey I have come to know, as we make our way into the Senior Center, called Little House, one morning. A few of our friends from our apartment complex have asked to come to Zumba with us. We have our own little entourage, as we parade through the Senior Center.

Coco, our petite, energetic friend from China, loves our class and has also invited some friends. Lori, from Texas is a former model. Sally, who is from England, and worked with Abbey at the newspaper, meets us at the entrance to the building. We are the cool kids, a collection of women, different sizes, shapes, and nationalities. We all love the music and dancing, but Abbey is the catalyst who has brought us all together.

We are swinging and shimmying to the fiery, Latin music. We are sexy and sultry, shaking our moneymakers, as our teacher likes to say. Suddenly, the door opens and a woman with a camera comes into the room.

Everyone stops dancing at once. We are shy and self-conscious. She tells us that she is doing a story for the local newspaper and needs to take some photos. We scuttle to the back of the room. "No, no, please don't take my picture," we are all protesting. Abbey shakes her head in disbelief at all of us clumped together.

"You can take my picture," Abbey tells the photographer.

She walks to the front of the room and strikes a pose. The rest of us agree to start dancing again, but only if the photographer avoids shooting any embarrassing booty shots. As I watch Abbey dancing, I wonder if she was always so fearless. Maybe I need to care less about what other people think of me. The photographer says she thinks our pictures will be on the cover of the weekly town newspaper. This should be a good test of my new "care-less" attitude.

The Return of the Prodigal Stuff

When we get back to Abbey's apartment that night, a miracle has occurred. The prodigal stuff from storage has returned. To Abbey, it is a joyous family reunion. Her father's desk is stuffed with the architectural blueprints he created and his handwritten notes. She shows me his tools, his drawings, and the stuff he used in his life. Her mother's jewelry and clothing are lovingly stroked by Abbey.

Her beloved furniture has come home. It is a treasure chest of memories. Boxes of photographs hold the key to family, friends, and happy times. To me, it doesn't look like much. To Abbey, it is boundless joy. I watch Abbey holding her father's notebook. He was an artist, and his sketches are alive on these pages. One picture shows a church that he built nestled into the woodland surroundings. A stained-glass lamp shade reminds Abbey of past homes and family. These things are her connection to people and places that she may not be able to remember. Sometimes stuff is so much more than just stuff.

Chapter 6 May

May Day, May Day
or
What's Love Got To Do With It?

One day, we are out walking around Palo Alto, and we find ourselves in front of a curious sight. The two-story house is multicolored, and the surrounding yard is exploding with art, statues, and indescribable objects.

"I wanted to show you this house," Abbey says to me.

As we are absorbing all the wonder, I notice an older black man trimming the bushes.

"Hi. Do you live here?" I ask.

He laughs, "Usually, people assume I'm the gardener and they ask me how much I charge. I tell them I get to sleep with the woman who owns the house, so I work for free." We all laugh. I think we have just made a new friend.

We introduce ourselves, and Henry tells us how he came to live in this marvelous mansion. He was the first black professional football player at a time when segregation was still the norm. He was not allowed to eat with the team and had to sleep separately from the other players.

The Secret Friend

When he met Rochelle, a white woman, he fell deeply in love with her. However, inter-racial couples were not accepted and actually against the law in most states. The coach said he could not date a white woman and play football. Henry was told he would have to choose between the game he adored and the woman he loved. He chose Rochelle and his football career ended. It's been over 50 years, the world has changed, and he has never regretted his decision.

"She's the love of my life," he says, "She is also an artist. She loves unconventional art. In fact, she works right here."

"Can we meet her?" Abbey asks.

"Sure, follow me." We quickly fall in behind this charming man as he leads us over to a converted garage.

"Rochelle, you've got some visitors," he calls through the open door.

A pretty woman comes out to greet us. She is gracious and welcoming. Her feelings for Henry are still obvious as she smiles and touches his arm gently. "Hello. Did Henry tell you our story?"

"He did," Abbey says, "I really like it."

"Come on in and I will show you what I do," she says. Rochelle's studio is an odd mix of delicate jewelry and colossal pieces of fused metal. We follow her into their home, where she tells us almost everything is for sale.

Her approach to stuff is different from the norm. She takes her own stuff and other people's stuff, makes it into something new, and then sends it back out into the world again. She is not attached to stuff.

She likes to recycle objects and create spectacular pieces of art. To create this amazing collection, she uses a blowtorch to weld discarded objects into dazzling visual treats. Unconventional art, an unusual approach to life, and an atypical love story; I know we are somewhere very special. Rochelle and Henry are an incredible example of the persistence and power of love. As we are leaving, Rochelle invites us back for her open studio tour. I know we will be back. "This is what sacrifice and true love look like," I think to myself.

How Many Opinions Make a Difference?

That night, I receive an email from John. He would like my input regarding Abbey. Her doctor wants to meet with her to assess her condition. I pounce on the opportunity to voice my opinion. If my loved one was suffering with a challenging medical condition, I would scoop them up and exhaust every possible option available. I suggest sweeping Abbey up and taking her to the Mayo Clinic for a complete evaluation. Check her in for a month, let them test her for everything, see if there are any biochemical imbalances, tumors, or some overlooked cause for her symptoms. Ask her doctor if he would consider referring her to a holistic center for another diagnosis.

John's answer is clear, "I don't want a second opinion."

I'm confused and disappointed. I think if this was my loved one, I would go to infinity and beyond to save them. I would make whatever sacrifice was necessary to save their life and make them well again. I would pound on doors, demand answers, and explore even the most radical treatments. I've confronted similar dilemmas with my children's health, and I'm pretty sure I would do almost anything to save them.

John calls me after the disastrous appointment with the doctor. He wants to talk to me, so we meet in my apartment lobby. Abbey hates the doctor and would not cooperate with any of the tests. The tears come pouring out. The doctor's prognosis is grim.

Early-Onset Alzheimer's is especially aggressive. Abbey is on a steep decline. It is no longer safe to leave her alone. The doctor has given John an idea of how Alzheimer's will devastate her mind and body. He told John that the disease will destroy her brain; she will lose her ability to walk, talk, and swallow. The doctor told John that Abbey has limited time left.

I can't help crying too. She is much too full of life to die. I am still hopeful that with more exercise, socialization, and time, she might at least go into remission. John shakes his head; he has accepted the doctor's timeline of events.

I'm just baffled. I see a woman who is capable of dancing on stages and attending professional conferences. John is talking about decline and death. We are looking at the same person, but what we see could not be more different. Maybe, I see what is still there and John is focusing on what has been lost.

I read about a health fair at Stanford University, and I plan a way for Abbey and me to "accidentally" discover it. It's in a building with glass walls, and we can see balloons, and a lot of people moving around. When we get inside, we find long tables staffed with experts in a variety of areas. I know that researchers from the Memory Clinic are going to be there, and we make our way to their table.

Once Abbey sees the literature on Alzheimer's, she gets a bit defensive. Looking directly at the researcher, she tells him, "I have Alzheimer's. I hate my doctor and the medicine doesn't work." I wonder how often the researchers are approached by individuals with Alzheimer's.

140

The Secret Friend

In fact, I think it is probably unusual for someone with Abbey's level of difficulties to be attending health fairs, and a lot of the other places we go.

Several of the other people behind the table move closer to talk to Abbey. "We have a lot of new medicines, and we could help you find a new doctor if you wanted us to help."

"Yes, my doctor doesn't listen to me," she says.

"You seem to be doing really well," the man at the booth says.

Abbey is flattered, "Thanks. I can do everything."

They are looking at me, "Are you her daughter?"

"I'm Abbey's friend," I say, "If you have any information, we would love to bring it home."

I look at Abbey, "That way you and John can read it together."

Abbey is already busy taking brochures and flyers. "How can I get in touch with you?" she asks the researchers. We leave with a bag of information.

"Abbey, I would be happy to take you to meet any of the doctors," I say.

"Thanks," she says, "John can help me. That's John's job."

I send John an email telling him all about our encounter with the Alzheimer's researchers. I am not surprised by his answer, "Thanks, I will look at the material, but Abbey already has an excellent doctor."

Susan Bostian

When Wonderland Beckons

The next day, Abbey and I are back at Starbucks sipping our coffee. I casually mention that I have heard that there's something fun happening at Alice's Restaurant up in the mountains.

"I've been there." Abbey tells me. "I used to date this guy who drove a motorcycle, and we would drive up to Alice's together."

"There's a theater group that likes to perform outdoors. They are performing Alice in Wonderland in the woods this year, and they are giving a little preview today."

"That could be fun," Abbey agrees, "let's go check it out."

By the time we drive up the mountain, the air temperature has dropped. Luckily, I have extra clothes in the car, and I give Abbey a heavy leather jacket to wear. Motorcycles outnumber cars in the parking lot. The clientele is a mix of wealthy tech titans, biker dudes, and regular folks.

Today, however, the crowd has become a little more diverse. The Cheshire Cat and his friends are stalking around the grounds. Abbey and I join the group sitting at the outdoor tables. A man wearing a tuxedo and top hat steps forward to welcome us to Wonderland.

"I hope they say the part about the pelican," Abbey says loudly.

The announcer smiles at Abbey, and with a dramatic flourish says, "What a wondrous bird is the pelican. His beak can hold more than his belly can." Abbey is delighted.

The characters take turns standing up and reading bits of Alice's famous story aloud. After the show is over, the White Rabbit comes over to talk with us. "Have you seen any of our shows?"

"I've seen all of them," Abbey announces proudly.

"Wow, what's your name?" asks the White Rabbit.

"Abbey."

The White Rabbit calls to the Alice character, "Hey, come meet Abbey. She's been to all of our shows."

I'm pretty sure that Abbey has never been to any of their performances. This is starting to feel a bit surreal. Alice comes skipping over.

"That's awesome," Alice tells Abbey.

Alice looks at me, "Have you seen all of our shows?"

"Actually, I haven't. This was my first time," I admit sheepishly.

Abbey looks at Alice, "She needs to get out more. I have to show her a lot of things."

The Cheshire Cat springs into our group, "Which one is Abbey?"

"I am," she says proudly.

144

The Secret Friend

The Cheshire Cat grins at her, "Would you like to come to our tea party?"

Abbey links arms with the Cheshire Cat and they sashay across the grass to the buffet table. The cast members offer us little cakes and tea. Abbey has become the guest of honor. We are chatting away. Abbey's answers all seem to make sense. She is a super fan and a super star.

We are all laughing, enjoying the moment and having a normal conversation at Alice's Restaurant with Alice in Wonderland, and sipping tea with the Cheshire Cat. What could be more normal than that?

Personally, I think spending some time in Wonderland might be good medicine. Wonderland was full of magic. And right now, we could all use a little magic.

I'm sort of chuckling to myself, when I realize I probably look a bit crazy, laughing at nothing in particular.

Then, I look around and decide that if you're at a tea party in Wonderland, laughing at nothing makes absolute sense. The White Rabbit is looking pretty cute. I wonder if he's single.

Chapter 7 June

Once in a Lifetime

John wants to meet to discuss some important issues. I've just worked 16 days in a row. For most of May, I have been working fifty-three or more hours a week. At first, John suggests a decrease in hours and a raise in pay, or just keeping the pay at $1000 a week. I'm not sure what he's suggesting. We both agree that we are tired. We also acknowledge that this is costing him a lot of money, but the alternatives are even more expensive. I don't have any answers.

There is one pot of money for John and Abbey. One of them does not have much time to live. One of them requires extra care. One of them will outlive the other and need to live on the remainder of the money.

Where should the money be spent? Does it matter where the money came from? If the money is Abbey's inheritance, is she entitled to more of it?

According to Abbey's sister, John has made a lot of sacrifices in his life for Abbey. Does that mean he has earned a larger share of the pot? As John would say, "this is all new territory."

John seems unusually enthusiastic when he comes to my apartment to pay me. "I have big news," he says. I'm wondering if he is now willing to explore different medical scenarios for Abbey.

"I have been offered a once in a lifetime opportunity to sail from San Francisco to Hawaii in the Pacific Sailboat Race. I would be on a boat with a really accomplished group of sailors."

I must be frowning, because he adds, "This has been a life dream of mine. It's part of my five-year life plan." Under normal circumstances, well, if these were normal circumstances, we wouldn't be having this conversation.

"What about Abbey?"

"I told her about it, and she said she wants me to go. I also told her sister, and she thinks I should go too. But I wanted to know what you thought."

"If you are asking for my opinion, then, honestly, I would say no. You are her sun and her moon. You are her life rhythm, her lifeline. If she is terminal, and she only has a short time before she dies, I would say stay with her. Go next time, when she is not alive, or aware. She still knows what's going on."

"I feel really guilty about that, but I will never have this chance again."

"Is this the only time the race is being held?"

"Well, it only happens every other year."

"So, you could go two years from now?"

"Yes, but probably not with this boat and these sailors."

This is not sounding much like a once in a lifetime opportunity to me. Abbey is running out of life, and being with her sounds like the real once in a lifetime opportunity. If he needs to postpone his life dreams, then that seems like the logical sacrifice to me.

"Everyone else thinks I should go. I really need a break and this would be good for me."

"I don't know how she would survive without you." I'm thinking how difficult it was for her when he was only gone for one night.

"Would you be willing to help?"

"How long would you be gone?"

"There's a significant commitment of time, if I join the crew. The race will probably take about two weeks of sailing. There would be weekend practices, and all-day seminars I would need to attend before the race. I have to let them know soon if I'm going to do this."

"I really don't think this is a good idea."

"I'm probably going to do it," he says. It's suddenly clear to me that he is not really asking for my opinion. He has already made the decision to go.

"I will help, but I can't do it alone. I'm still Abbey's friend. I can't suddenly move in with her and spend every day and night with her for two weeks."

"I would hire someone to spend nights with her."

"She won't accept a caregiver."

"Do you know anyone who would do this?"

"Maybe. My sister, Nancy, might be available, but I think you still need to get someone else to help. I will work with the agency to introduce the caregiver as a friend."

"Great, ask your sister if she will help. I've got the name of an agency and I'll call them today."

I have a terrible feeling about this plan.

Linda calls me that night. "I told him he should go," she says, "He really deserves a break. He's done a lot for my sister. He needs to take care of himself too. I'll come out and visit for a couple of days while he's gone."

My sister is thrilled with the idea of coming to California. "I'm happy that I am going to get to meet Abbey and spend time with her," she tells me.

Nancy is also excited about working and making some money while staying with me. It looks like I'm the only one who doesn't think this is a good idea.

John talks with an agency and they recommend a woman named, Rachel, to stay with Abbey during the night. The manager of the agency and I talk about our unusual arrangement working as a secret friend. I tell her that whoever takes this job must agree not to divulge this secret. I tell her about Abbey's likes, dislikes, and routines. I give her my number, so that I can coordinate with the caregiver.

Rachel, the new caregiver, and I come up with a plan to "accidentally" run into each other at Starbucks. I introduce Rachel to Abbey as my friend. The meeting goes well. We talk about our kids and Abbey seems to like Rachel. A couple of days later, we all meet for an enjoyable lunch. Maybe we will be able to pull this off.

Meanwhile, the Almanac runs the story about Senior Center and the Zumba class. Unfortunately, they refer to our class as Rhumba, instead of Zumba. This completely defeats the purpose of presenting the Senior Center as hip and cool. The Zumba teacher is outraged and wants the newspaper to come back and do another story.

No one else seems to care about the little typo. Most of our Senior Center friends think we are amazing. We did a funny little dance, and our pictures are in the newspaper.

Abbey and I return to the newspaper offices to get extra copies of the article. They have run a photo of our class, but we are tucked inside the newspaper, not on the front page. When I see the photo, I am relieved to see that I am in the background. When Abbey sees the photo, she wants to know why it's not bigger. I think there are as many versions of reality as there are perspectives.

Just Trying to Stay Afloat

June passes quickly. Like ducks swimming on a pond, we are smooth and serene on the surface, but the part that cannot be seen is paddling like crazy. Abbey and I attend Zumba, visit Ray, check in with our rock-guy, Preston, dance with Felton, go to lunch with Coco, attend pottery shows, hike new trails, chase some peacocks around a state park, and socialize with the other residents of our apartment complex. Our routine is stimulating and comforting.

One evening, after a long day, I come through the door and barely greet my son. I trip over one of the unpacked boxes, as I fall down onto my sofa bed.

"What's wrong with you?" my son wants to know.

"I'm just really tired," I say.

"From what?" my son asks.

"From working."

"Working? How can you be tired? You get paid to go out for coffee with someone," my son says incredulously.

"That's what you see, but there's much more to it than that."

Behind the scenes, I am coordinating with the agency, advising the new "friend," planning my sister's trip, and designing a two-week live performance, with real life consequences. If things deteriorate, I want to know who to call. If things really fall apart, I realize I will have to bring Abbey to the hospital, or call 911. My goal has always been that nothing bad will happen to her on my watch, and I don't want this to be an exception.

CHAPTER 8 JULY

Bon Voyage, Happy Trails, and Vessels in the Night

The big day arrives, and we all take our places. I think Abbey will have a better understanding of John's absence if we take him to the marina, and she watches him get on the sailboat. John swings by our apartment to pick me up. Abbey is sitting in the front seat, happy to see me. But, I am not alone.

"Abbey, look who came to visit me," I say, "This is my sister, Nancy. She flew in last night to surprise me. She's just like me, except she's a better version."

Abbey looks her over, "She does look like you, except she's prettier." My sister gasps, but I smile. I'm used to Abbey's blunt honesty.

We chat about the sailboat race on the way to the marina. I want to reinforce the image of John on a boat, so I ask, "Why would eight men want to get on a boat and sail across the ocean without even being able to take a shower?"

We all laugh and Abbey says, "That doesn't sound like fun to me."

I ask endless questions about the trip, "Is it going to be cold on the boat? Do you have to take turns getting up in the middle of the night and sail in the dark? Whose idea was this?"

Abbey asks Nancy if she has been to California before. "A long time ago, but I don't remember much about it."

Abbey is pleased, "I can show you a lot of places. I grew up here."

Nancy plays along perfectly, "Abbey, I would really like you to show me around."

I think we are off to a great start. We talk about how much fun we are going to have together, while John is gone. I am setting the stage for the next 14 days.

"John, we will try to follow the race on the internet, but we might be having too much fun to check very often." We take turns teasing John about the race.

"Yeah, too bad you're going to be cold and miserable, John."

"Hey, John, don't pee into the wind."

Abbey giggles, "I'm going to spend a lot of money while you are on your boat."

John seems a little anxious. I'm not sure if it is because of the two weeks at sea, or the three women at home with a credit card. I'm feeling pretty confident that Abbey will get almost anything she wants while he is away.

We arrive at the yacht club in the Alameda, and John introduces us to the other sailors and their significant others. Most of the sailors have wives or girlfriends who will meet them in Hawaii after the race. At one point, we discussed the possibility of someone flying to Hawaii with Abbey. Ultimately, the idea was dismissed, although I don't remember why. The after race parties

154

are infamous and will continue for days after the last sailors finish the course.

John is unsure when he will return. At this point I think if he is going to participate in the race, he might as well enjoy a couple of days of festivities, but it will all depend on how well things are going at home with Abbey.

We stick around long enough to watch the boat motor away from the dock. It is a rather unceremonious departure, and it gives me an idea.

"Hey, the starting line is at the St. Francis Yacht Club in San Francisco," I say, "Let's go meet John at the Yacht Club. Then we can see the actual race begin."

We have nothing but time, and I really want to give Abbey a sense of where John has gone. Plus, John has given us the big, blue BMW to drive while he is gone. Abbey is really fond of this car. It belonged to her father. The BMW was bequeathed to John and Abbey after her father passed away.

Abbey and Nancy want to see John one more time before he leaves, so we motor over the Bay Bridge. Abbey is excited about surprising John. This time there are more boats, and sailors, and we wander around the prestigious yacht club as if we belonged there.

John is quite amazed to see us. He brings us down to the boat and we say our goodbyes again. This time, John and Abbey both seem quite emotional. There are lots of hugs and kisses, and a few tears. We take a few photos and John thanks us again for coming to see him off. Then, it is time for him to leave.

The actual race begins in front of the Golden Gate Bridge, and I know just the spot to watch the boats sail by. I drive the short distance, and we jump out of the car and run down to the water's edge. We are almost underneath the towering bridge. We have a spectacular view of the sailboats, their gorgeous sails billowing in the wind. All the boats look the same to us, so we wave our arms and shout in their general direction.

"Go John, go!" "Win the race!" "Beat the other boats!" "Get to Hawaii before the other boats!" "Goodbye, John" "Win John, win!"

The three of us are definitely the strangest cheering squad for the famous sailboat race, but I don't care. We have our own race to run, and we have just crossed the starting line with John. I am determined to finish successfully, and Abbey will be the winner.

Slipping Down The Devil's Slide

"I'm cold," Abbey says.

"I'm hungry," Nancy adds.

"All right, lunch at the Warming Hut, and then we will go off on an adventure." I turn to Abbey. "You worked here with your dad, didn't you?"

"Yup, I worked here and at Alcatraz," she says.

Nancy smiles, "That's really cool, Abbey. My sons came out to California and wanted to go to Alcatraz, but Susan said it would be too scary." She looks directly at me, "They have never forgotten this."

I shake my head and look at Abbey, "You were so smart not to have children. They just make you crazy."

"I used to be sad that I didn't have kids, but now I'm happy that I don't. Let's get something to eat."

After lunch, we head out to a quaint town of Pacifica, overlooking the Pacific Ocean. The fog is clearing as we arrive and the sun comes out shining brightly. Last night, I found a couple of garage sales and one estate sale advertised on Craig's list for this area. We stop at the estate sale first and it's a disappointment. I tell Nancy that we are never sure what we are going to find, some places are interesting, some are duds.

"But, we keep looking," Abbey tells her. "Some of them are really good." Our next stop is a garage sale, but we are having trouble finding it. Just as we are about to give up, I spot a small sign in front of a little house.

From the outside, it doesn't look like much, and we almost don't get out of the car. But, I see some tables with sea shells and a man standing by himself. If nothing else, we can have a conversation with him. As we approach the tables, I find myself looking at a gorgeous collection of beautiful shells.

The man greets us and invites us to ask him any questions. We want to know where and how he has collected this many sea shells. He tells us that he has collected shells for his entire life. He has traveled around the world to find certain specimens and he also trades with other collectors.

Since we are so interested in sea shells, he offers to show us his special collection. He raises the garage door, and I would swear we were standing in a museum. He has glass shelves lining all the walls from the floor to the ceiling. He has glass cases in the middle of the garage showcasing the some of the most exotic shells I have ever seen in my life. We are speechless.

"I have more inside my home. My wife says we don't have any more space, so I can't collect any more shells. I'm selling some of these so I can get some new ones." The designs and colors are exquisite.

"I have been to a lot of aquariums and museums," I tell him, "and I have never seen anything like this."

He gives us the tour of the collection, pointing out rare and fascinating shells. We are mesmerized. Abbey wants to know

158

where the shells were found and he is happy to take us on a tour of the world through sea shells. I'm not a marine biologist, but I'm pretty sure this is an outstanding collection. Some of these shells are humongous.

Abbey points to a bright orange shell. "Are you selling that one? I really like the color."

"If you want it, I'll give it to you," he says smiling at her. Abbey is thrilled and accepts immediately.

Nancy's dilemma is how to ship all the shells she wants back home. I find a delicate white shell with pink tips. We know that we have found something very special and we each want to take a piece of it home with us.

The man sweetly agrees to take our pictures in front of the spectacular sea shells. When we get back into the car, I look back at the unassuming little place. He has closed the garage door. Sometimes, there is so much more hidden inside. I'm glad we took the time to look.

I have planned our trip so that we will drive south on Route 1, beside the Pacific Ocean. The views are spectacular. We drive along the narrow road by the ocean, rising and dipping, in awe of the sparkling, endless body of water, so close to our car. Life on the edge, dazzling, unpredictable, peaks and valleys; we are traveling between the warning signs for unstable ground and dangerous cliffs.

This part of the drive is called Devil's Slide. Bright yellow signs warn us of falling rocks interspersed with signs warning us about treacherous cliffs. We are cruising along the edge of a cliff, between the falling rocks and the steep drop onto jagged rocks.

I look over at Abbey, sitting in the front seat next to me. We have the windows down, the breeze is blowing her hair around her face, and her elbow is leaning out the window. Her face has the look of a contented queen, surveying her surroundings, and pleased with her kingdom. I don't know what will happen on our journey, the obstacles are enormous, and the dangers are real, but I'm going to try to keep her safe and serene.

Turbulence Ahead

Our next stop is Half Moon Bay. We walk barefoot on the beach, we eat chowder at Sam's Chowder House, and listen to the live band playing songs. The day feels close to perfection. We are sitting in beach chairs around a fire pit, sipping hot chocolate, when my cell phone buzzes, notifying me of a text message. Rachel wants to know what time we are bringing Abbey home.

"Give us an hour and we will meet you back at the house," I text her back.

"Abbey knows I'm from the agency. John talked to me about it in front of her yesterday," she writes back.

"What?!!" I'm banging the letters onto my phone, but I'm trying to look calm.

"I know. Abbey got really upset and started screaming and crying. She didn't want me there."

"Omg." I can't believe it. "Why would he do that?"

"He said she already knew."

I look over at Abbey. She is peaceful, chatting with Nancy. Why would John have told Abbey that Rachel was a caregiver after all my efforts to introduce her as a friend?

Was John trying to make this situation more difficult during his absence? Whatever his motives, he is gone now, and I have to handle the situation alone. This was one time I hoped that Abbey might forget.

We arrive back at Abbey's apartment and discover Rachel already sitting inside. Abbey looks disturbed by her presence. "I don't want her here," she says to me.

"Let's all sit down and talk about it," I say. Maybe we can smooth this over. "Hi Rachel, what's going on?"

"I brought some music for us to listen to," Rachel says, "Abbey, do you like music?" Abbey sits down next to me and refuses to answer. Any hope that she would not remember dissolves instantly.

"Maybe we could all watch a movie together," I suggest. No one really wants to do this, but I don't have a plan B. I turn on the television, and pretend to be very enthusiastic about the program.

The movie ends at 10 o'clock. Nancy is falling asleep on the sofa. Rachel looks cranky and Abbey has not left my side.

"Abbey, I have to take Nancy home, and put her to bed, but we will be back early in the morning to get you. Would you like to go out to breakfast with us?"

"Yes, come back early for me," she says. She looks so vulnerable that I think I might cry if I stay any longer.

I give her a hug. "Ok, wait for us here at the apartment. We will see you soon. Good night."

Nancy and I barely get back to my apartment when my phone buzzes. It is a text from Rachel, "She didn't say anything to me. She just climbed into her bed with her clothes on."

162

"Don't disturb her," I reply, "Maybe things will be better in the morning. Call me if anything goes wrong during the night."

I'm Alright, You're Alright, We're All Alright, Right?

The next morning, Abbey is waiting on the steps. She is staring at each car as it goes by. Rachel is waiting nearby, but they are not talking with each other.

"Good morning, Abbey!" I say. She looks relieved to see me.

"I'm ready to go," she says. She walks away from Rachel without saying a word.

"How are you?" I ask, even though I think I already know the answer.

"I don't want that woman here. I don't need her," she says. She is starting to cry.

"Is she just going to stay with you at night?" I ask innocently.

"John is paying her to take care of me. Did you know about this?" She looks directly at me.

We have 13 days to go, and I do not want her to be mad at me.

"No, I'm shocked that he would do such a thing." My goal is to keep her safe and happy. John may have blown the cover, but I am not going to deal with the fallout.

"Abbey, should we take Nancy to the dog park?" I ask, changing the subject, "We can talk about this while we are walking around."

The Secret Friend

"Abbey, will you show me what to do at the dog park?" Nancy is playing her role perfectly.

"Yes, the dogs are friendly," she says. I think the distraction technique is working.

As we stroll among the frisky four legged friends, Abbey is pleased to show Nancy how to make friends with the dogs. We greet several familiar faces and their furry friends.

After an hour of petting pooches, we find we are suddenly hungry. We head over to our favorite breakfast place. "Good morning, Abbey!" says the hostess. I can't help smiling. Abbey is walking through the restaurant like a celebrity.

Showing Nancy around California seems to appeal to Abbey. "Let's bring Nancy over to meet Ray." I think this is a great idea. Abbey and I both gush about Ray's virtues.

Ray impresses all of us with his knowledge about birds, bees, and flowers. We introduce Nancy and he gives us the grand tour of the grounds. Ray gives some birdseed to Abbey who is beaming as the chickens crowd around her. The rooster crows disapprovingly as his chickens happily follow Abbey around the yard.

A strange looking creature appears. Ray introduces us to the beekeeper who is in full bee keeping regalia. Abbey remembers a recent incident where John was frightened by a bee. "He screamed when he saw the bee," she says laughing.

"Don't bring him around here," says the beekeeper, "We have 100,000 bees in the hive back there."

"Yes, and the bees get agitated when the temperature is over 90 degrees," adds Ray. Ray's expertise is limitless.

The beekeeper promises to bring jars of honey for us the next time he comes back. We have a growing circle of places and people who know us and greet us by name. Abbey is part of an expanding network of friends and connections.

We spend the rest of the day introducing Nancy to our favorite people and places, the town's community farm, the duck pond, and the shorelines. We end our day laughing over a delicious dinner.

As we are reflecting on our wonderful day, we talk about how cold, wet, and miserable John must be sitting on his little boat. I hope this will accomplish several things: it reminds us that John is on his boat and not coming home tonight, we are having fun, Abbey has a strong support system, and she is well enough to survive without him until he returns. Considering the rocky start, our day has been amazingly successful. I hope that Abbey's positive mood will carry over into the evening when Rachel shows up again.

Nothing's Wrong, but Nothing's Right

Abbey's happiness starts to fade as we drive up to the apartment. "I hope that woman isn't here," she says, "I don't like her at all."

I have been exchanging text messages all day with Rachel. My advice; reinforce our friend connections, don't act like a caregiver, be more like a helpful friend. Before we leave the restaurant, I send a text to Rachel telling her to wait in her car for us, not in the apartment.

As I park in front of Abbey's apartment, Rachel runs over to us and opens Abbey's car door. At first, I think Abbey is not going to get out of the car.

"Let's bring all of our stuff inside," I say encouragingly.

I have decided to act as though everything is going well.

"We had a wonderful day, Rachel. How are you?"

"Good. I brought over some music for us to listen to tonight."

"Oh, nice," I say, "We love music, don't we, Abbey?"

"Yes," Abbey responds unenthusiastically. We spend some more time talking about our fun day before we leave. Abbey is moving around the apartment. She seems to be looking for something.

"Abbey, thank you for a wonderful time today, I'm going to take Nancy down to the hot tub. If you and Rachel want to join us, we can meet you there."

Nancy also thanks Abbey. We exchange hugs. "Let's take Nancy to some more fun places tomorrow, okay?" Abbey is hesitant, but agrees.

We manage to get to the car and drive back to my apartment, before my phone rings. Rachel is panicking,

"Abbey won't stay with me. She told me to get out, and then she ran away."

"Where is she now?" I ask, "You're following her, right?"

"She said she was going to the pool to find you."

"OK, you need to follow her and stay with her until we get there. We'll be right over."

Nancy overhears the conversation. "She is never going to stay with that woman," she says.

"Ok, let's go figure this out." We throw on our bathing suits and as we dash over to the hot tub, I see Abbey standing on the balcony of the clubhouse. Rachel is standing about ten feet away from her. We wave and Abbey comes rushing down to meet us. She is still wearing her dress and the tears are streaming down her face.

Without hesitation, Abbey walks right down the stairs into the hot tub, the black and white dress billowing in the water around her. "I don't want her. There's nothing wrong with me."

The other people in the hot tub are staring, and my heart is breaking for her. Rachel is off to the side talking on her cell phone. Abbey is now standing in the middle of the hot tub, fully

168

dressed and crying. "I don't need her. There's nothing wrong with me."

I give her a hug. "I'm so sorry. Let's sit down and talk about it." We are already wet, I think we might as well stay warm in the hot tub.

"Why did John do this to me?" she says.

I have to find a way to make this work.

"Maybe John asked her to stay with you, because he loves you so much. So Rachel is here to make John feel good. So he doesn't have to worry while he is on his trip," I say.

I'm trying to re-frame this scenario to make it more acceptable to Abbey.

I agree that she is fine, even though she is sitting in the hot tub in a dress. A couple is sitting across from us watching the drama unfold. They're not even trying to be discreet about it. They are staring wide eyed at us, their heads moving back and forth as if they were at a tennis match. For the next hour, we agree that Abbey really doesn't need anyone, but maybe, John needs Rachel to stay at the apartment. Abbey seems to accept this explanation.

Finally, Abbey has calmed down and I'm starting to feel more optimistic about the night. I tell Abbey that we will pick her up in the morning and we will all go out for coffee. We climb out of the hot tub and I put my towel around Abbey.

"I'll see you in the morning." I start to walk away, when Abbey calls to me.

"Wait, I need to talk with you."

We move over to a table and sit down. Abbey starts sobbing, and says she just cannot go home with that woman.

"I don't want a stranger to stay in my house," she says, "Why would John do that to me?"

"Can you just let Rachel stay at your house for tonight? You don't need to talk to her, just let her sleep over?"

She starts to get more upset. "You don't understand. I don't want that woman in my house."

"Abbey, for safety reasons, you have to have someone sleep over in case there is an emergency during the night."

"Can I sleep at your house?"

I hesitate, considering the lack of space. "Um, I don't have any beds. I sleep on the sofa."

She looks around. "Can Nancy stay with me?" She seems to be pleading with me.

I call Nancy over and Abbey asks her directly, "Can you sleep over with me?"

"Sure, of course, Abbey, I would love to stay at your place with you."

Abbey looks at Rachel, and then at me, "Will you tell her?"

I can't even begin to imagine how desperate and difficult this must be for her. "Yes, don't worry, I'll explain it to Rachel."

170

The Secret Friend

I call Rachel over and explain the situation. Rachel seems relieved and agrees that this is probably the best solution. She has been on the phone talking to the director from the agency. The metal gate slams loudly as she leaves.

We take Abbey home, get her settled, and tucked into bed. Nancy climbs into the bed in the guest room.

"Nancy, I'll come back for you in the morning. But, call me right away if there are any problems."

Abbey comes storming down the hall. She is all upset. "Are we going to have to go through all this again?" she says.

"What?" I say, shocked.

"That woman, I don't want her in my house."

"Abbey, it's Nancy. You asked her to stay with you." I turn the light on so she can see Nancy.

"Hi Abbey, it's me, Nancy. You wanted me to sleep here."

Once Abbey sees Nancy, she calms down. "I thought that Rachel was back. Nancy is ok." She smiles. "All right. Good night." She walks back down the hall to her bedroom.

I decide it's a good time to exit, "We really need to get some sleep. I'll see you both in the morning."

I pick Abbey and Nancy up early the next morning. We begin our day by counting the days on the race calendar and checking John's location on the internet. Then, we go to Berkeley and give Nancy the happy, hippie tour.

On the way home, I veer off the highway, back toward Half Moon Bay. We visit Abbey's favorite pottery studio and eat dinner by the sea again. Still energetic, we go to the movies and laugh through a comedy. The movie ends, and Abbey becomes very quiet and starts fidgeting. I ask her if anything is wrong.

"I just can't take that woman again. Is she going to be at my apartment?" she asks.

"Abbey, I promise you, no one is going to be at your apartment."

"Nancy, are you going to stay with me?"

"Abbey, I'm going to stay with you until John gets back from his sailing trip."

Staying The Course

The next day, I pick Abbey and Nancy up again and bring them back to my apartment. Nancy jumps into the shower, while Abbey and I stare at the computer screen. We look at the tiny icons and locate John's position in the race.

We walk over to the clubhouse for brunch and chat with our friends. Nancy joins us and we go to a glass and pottery fair. After several hours of browsing through the beautiful works of art, we drive out to Woodside and eat salads at the Woodside Bakery. We return home and sit by the pool. After some consideration we go to the movie at the clubhouse. The movie is funny and Abbey appears relaxed. We walk back to Abbey's apartment and get her settled. She and Nancy seem to be developing a nighttime routine and Abbey seems very happy with Nancy.

For the next ten days, we sail through the days and nights, parallel to John, trying to finish the race successfully, trying desperately not to capsize, or sink. Each night, I design the following day's adventures. We fill our days with pottery shows, museums, consignment shops, movies, music, botanical gardens, and estate sales.

Every morning, Abbey comes to my apartment and we look at my computer. I load up the virtual race course and point to the small icon on the screen, "Look, Abbey, that's John's boat. He is in the lead."

"Yay, John! You better win." She is happy that her man is winning the race. I look for any news about the race. Some of the boats are posting videos and we watch the crews get tossed around by the rough waves. We watch the tiny boats crawl across the screen, closer to the virtual blob that is Hawaii. It is our ritual. I hope that it makes the journey more real for Abbey, and in truth, it keeps us all on course.

Linda comes to visit and we all get a chance to bond. We go out for coffee and bring Abbey's sister to Zumba. Abbey gets a chance to dance wildly and show her sister how much fun we have at Zumba. Linda and I finally have a chance to talk while Abbey and Nancy are chatting.

"I haven't seen Abbey this happy since she was four years old," Linda says.

Linda tells me that Abbey was always prickly, and even as a child, no one wanted to be around her.

I wonder if Alzheimer's could have affected her personality from the beginning of her life. What if the prickles were early signs of the tangles of Alzheimer's? What if something sticky, like plaque, had permanently disabled her filter? What if all her thoughts just poured out uncontrollably and the disease had inactivated her ability to assess what was appropriate?

What if her difficult personality was the disease in stealth mode? How sad would it be if she had been judged harshly all her life and the disease had been the real offender? And which Abbey is real - the difficult, prickly, loner, that her sister has described, or the kind, extroverted, friend that I have come to know?

174

The Secret Friend

This trip has also made it clear that we need a backup person, another "friend" to jump into the mix when Nancy leaves. A friend tells me about a woman named Maria, who took care of her father when he was dying of Alzheimer's.

The woman is highly recommended and I explain our unique situation of being "Secret Friends." I tell her she must never divulge our secret and if she can play the role, we will bring her in as one of our new "friends." We "accidentally" meet for lunch and Abbey likes Maria immediately.

Susan Bostian

Lighting The Way

With each day, I am feeling more positive about winning this race. There just seems to be a lot of happiness around us, a light breeze is gently carrying us toward the finish line. Linda's visit has gone well, we have a new secret friend, and best of all Abbey is glowing with delight from all of our adventures.

Abbey is still acting as a tour guide for group. She wants to take Nancy to an estate sale, and I locate a promising one. As we enter the house, I see three women are running the sale. I don't recognize them as any of the usual organizers.

Abbey encourages Nancy to open drawers and look for treasures in the closets. I spot a Light Therapy Pole Lamp, which I have always wanted, priced at $50. Usually they cost at least a few hundred dollars. We walk upstairs and go through clothing, bedding, knick-knacks, and shoes. Abbey finds a hat sitting on a shelf in one of the bedrooms.

On the way downstairs, I notice a large collage of photographs of a young woman. As I look more closely, I realize I know her. She was one of my daughter's friends. She was smart, athletic, funny, and nice.

Tragically, she was killed in a freak accident. Suddenly, all the stuff takes on a different meaning. I approach the women selling the items.

"Is this your business to run estate sales?" I ask one of them.

"No," she responds.

"Are you friends of the family?"

"Yes."

They are not very forthcoming, so I explain that my daughter was a friend of the young girl, and I had met the mom a few times.

They start crying. They tell me the mom killed herself and left the house and stuff to them. They are too sad about it and just want to sell everything.

"What happened to the husband?" I ask.

"They divorced."

Now all the items are soaked with sadness. I look back at the lamp. For years, maybe even decades, I have wanted a light like this. This one is the deluxe model, free standing, maybe five or six feet tall, if you extend the accordion neck straight up to the ceiling. Despite the circumstances, I think this may be my only chance to own a super bright light like this. The price tag says $50. Even though I feel guilty, I ask if they will accept $25 and they agree.

I can't believe that I finally own the light that I have wanted so badly, for so long. Still, the tragic circumstances linger in my head. The horrible reality keeps replaying in my mind. Sometimes, things go so wrong for some people. I wonder if there is really any meaning to life, or it's just a random crap shoot. I'm leaning more toward random crap at this moment. I'm standing there with the crying women and there are just no words.

I look at all the other people who are still shopping blissfully unaware. Abbey wants the bright red hat and some utensils for the kitchen. Nancy chooses some small figurines. They look like they have come from Disney World, the happiest place on earth. There's some tragic irony here. Abbey and Nancy are still going through the stuff gleefully. But, for me, it's different knowing the previous owners of the stuff, and knowing how sadly it ended for them. We carry our new treasures back to the car. I'm hoping the clouds of tragedy will not follow us home with our new things.

That night, I sit down to write under the new light and let the brightness fill my head. I feel a bit unsettled as I think about the last woman who sat under this lamp.

My daughter comes through the door. "Where did you get that ugly lamp?"

I quickly tell her the sad story about the pictures of the friend, and the mother, and the women at the home. I explain how I have always wanted one of these lamps. For years, I have heard how wonderful they are for people who have Seasonal Affective Disorder, or depression.

Without hesitation, my daughter says, "Yeah, look how well it worked for her." And just like when the little voice said the emperor has no clothes, the light on the super lamp went dark.

Do any of us see things clearly or do we just see what we want to see? I think about the saying, "God never gives you more than you can handle." If that was true, this ugly lamp wouldn't be sitting in my apartment. It's more than I can deal with. I move the lamp to the back of my closet.

Ripples of Good

Somehow, time passes; we count the days on the calendar, we watch the race on the computer, we cheer John on from my apartment. We are strong, wild women, searching for adventures, dancing and playing with our friends.

More friends want to join us on the journey. Now, when we go to Zumba, my car is packed with "Zumba ladies." I drive, Abbey sits in front, Nancy, Coco, and Lori sit in the back seat. We are all in our colorful spandex, a rainbow of giddy parakeets chirping happily.

Abbey's friend, Sally, walks to class, and Coco's friend, Vivian, arrives a few minutes later. The music is intoxicating and we shimmy and shake together with wild abandon. Abbey is in the center of the room glowing brightly. We are all here enjoying ourselves because of Abbey. I am convinced that ripples of good have been generated from our benevolent deception.

Fourteen days pass.

Finally, it appears that the race is over, but the outcome is unclear. Ambiguity doesn't work for us, so we decree that John's boat has won his division. John calls Abbey on her cell phone and she is thrilled to hear his voice. She has been remarkably resilient, but I know she will be overjoyed by his return. Nancy wants to plan a romantic dinner for John and Abbey.

Abbey dismisses the idea. "We're not all mushy like that. We are friends and lovers."

The Secret Friend

Nancy seems a little disappointed. "We could still plan a nice dinner," she says, still trying to convince Abbey.

"I don't care about eating," she says, "We are going to be having wild sex in the bathtub, so don't call me."

Nancy looks surprised, but we are both amused and impressed. Abbey knows what she wants, and is not afraid to say it.

Secrets, Success, and Silver Sandals

We have enjoyed traveling in the luxurious BMW, and I'm a little sad about having to relinquish it. I also realize it might be a good idea to get it cleaned before John sees it again. We have spent a lot of time cruising around the bay area. I take it down to our local car wash. I'm waiting in line for the attendant to take the car. I start throwing away the accumulated trash.

As I pull some papers out from under the passenger's seat, a pair of silver sandals comes sliding out. I stare at them, trying to make sense of what I have found. They are very glittery, small, and totally unlike anything Abbey would wear. As the possibilities run through my mind, I stuff them back under the seat.

I call Nancy on her cell phone. She is sitting by the pool watching Abbey swim laps. As I describe the discovery, Nancy is not surprised. "I think most men would have someone on the side if their wives had a disease like this," she says.

"Maybe, we're jumping to conclusions," I tell her. "I'm going to ask Linda if she left her sandals in the car."

Linda is quick to respond to my email, "No, on the silver sandals (?)."

I relay the information back to Nancy with the suggestion, "Let's just not say anything about them."

We pick John up at the airport and he and Abbey are both emotional. I hand the keys to John and jump into the back seat with Nancy. I try to balance the conversation between listening to

182

John's story and encouraging Abbey to tell him how we had a wonderful time. I have already sent John the emails describing the Rachel debacle and we carefully avoid the subject.

Perhaps distance does make the heart grow fonder because there is a renewed tenderness between John and Abbey. John reaches across the front seat to hold Abbey's hand. They are very happy to see each other. John is relaxed and Abbey looks confident. They are the perfect picture of marital bliss. From my vantage point in the back seat, everything looks wonderful, except for the sparkly, silver sandals sitting directly beneath Abbey's seat.

I think we have all finished the race with a spectacular win. Nancy and I have just worked 24 hours a day for fourteen continuous days. We are exhausted from all the fun and fear. As they drop us off at my apartment, Abbey reminds us not to call her. We promise to wait to hear from her.

As we wearily climb the stairs, I tell Nancy, "I'm not going to set any alarm clocks."

"I would sleep through them, even if you did." Nancy says.

"I'm too tired to celebrate, but we did it," I say, "I'm not sure how we did it, but we kept her sane and safe."

"It was a miracle. I think it was fun, too," Nancy says, "But I'll know better when I'm awake."

I'm really proud of us, but the party is going to be brief. Nancy is flying back home in two days. I am feeling the pressure of being the only "secret friend." I really need Maria to work out.

Before Nancy leaves, John wants to talk with both of us. He is very appreciative of our efforts. His trip has been enormously fulfilling and he thanks us for making it possible for him to enjoy this experience. He has posted the pictures he took of us at the start of the race on a photo sharing site. I make a note to look them up later.

We are all impressed that Abbey allowed Nancy to stay with her. John thanks Nancy and asks if she would be willing to come back and help again for another trip. Despite the lack of sleep, Nancy says she would love to return again.

"John, there's a book you might like to read called, Jan's Story," says my sister innocently, "It's about Barry Peterson, his wife had Alzheimer's. He's been criticized for falling in love with another woman while his wife was still alive. But, I saw an interview with him on television and it was really interesting."

They continue discussing the delicate issue of taking lovers when a spouse has a disease or disability.

I am thinking of puzzles. Let's say a whole puzzle has a hundred pieces. If a few pieces of the puzzle are missing, does it stop being a puzzle? How many pieces need to be missing before it is something other than a puzzle?

What about people? How many pieces need to be missing before they are not a person? If marriage vows are until death, how much of a person needs to die, before the vows are void? When is it okay for silver sandals to move in?

184

John's phone rings and snaps me out of my pondering. Abbey is calling, wanting to know when he is coming home. She may not be all there, but she still has a lot of pieces left.

After John leaves, I tell Nancy, "I think you just gave him permission to have an extra marital affair."

We go back upstairs to my apartment. I want to see how we look in the photos we took on the docks.

We find the photo sharing website. John's profile pops up. There in bold letters, under the marital status, John has declared himself to be in an "open relationship."

"I guess he didn't need my permission," Nancy says.

CHAPTER 9 AUGUST

What is the Difference between Hope and False Hope?

We plan to have Maria show up to take Abbey out to lunch. I would like John to tell me his work schedule so we can plan accordingly.

He tells me, "It's hard for me to predict."

I am a bit frustrated. Abbey needs constant coverage and I'm really hoping that we can all work together to make this work. We finally find an afternoon for Maria to spend with Abbey.

That night, John sends me an email. "I don't think Abbey likes Maria. We will call you tomorrow morning."

The next morning, Abbey calls me to go out for coffee. As we settle into the car, I ask her about Maria.

Abbey acts uncomfortable, "I can't talk about it."

"Why? What happened?" I ask, concerned.

"She took me to her house. She works with her family, but I can't tell you about it."

"What kind of work do they do?"

Abbey seems frightened. "They take clothes to a warehouse. The big guys give me stuff for free, but I'm afraid of the big guys. I can't talk about them."

"What did they give you?"

"A dress, some stuff, but I don't want to talk about it."

When we get to Starbucks, I send a text message to John, "Did Abbey tell you she is afraid of some big guys she met with Maria?"

He responds, "Yes, but she often misinterprets situations."

I send a text message to the friend who recommended Maria. "Abbey says Maria gave her free stuff from a warehouse, and she is afraid of some big guys. Would Maria be involved in any illegal activities?"

She responds, "Haha. It wouldn't surprise me." I look at the text from my friend. Sometimes, I think, it's hard to tell who is not thinking clearly in this circle of friends.

I respond, "Really? Why would you recommend her to be with Abbey?"

"She was great with my dad when he had Alzheimer's. Her family just might have a little something going on the side."

At times like this, I am convinced of a couple of things. One, the Multi-verse could very easily exist. I am sitting across from Abbey who is completely unaware that I am communicating with other people while we are sitting there chatting. Two, if there is a line between reality and unreality, a lot of us drift back and forth across the lanes.

But, seriously, I am acutely aware of how vulnerable Abbey has become. Her perception may, or may not, be accurate and her ability to describe the situation is impaired. People are willing to doubt or dismiss her concerns because of her disease. I'm not sure about anything anymore.

Later that night, I call Maria. "Can you think of any reason why Abbey might be feeling afraid?" I ask her.

"No. Absolutely, not," says Maria, "She had a blast with me. I took her to consignment shops, and she bought some really cute things."

Now, I don't know what to believe.

"By the way," Maria informs me, "Abbey knows I'm being paid. John gave me money in front of her."

"Why would he do that?" I ask her.

"I don't know. Ask him."

I put a lot of time into establishing Maria as a mutual friend. I send John an email asking him for an explanation. The next day, I get John's response. "I didn't tell Abbey. Maria asked me to pay her in front of Abbey."

Dilemmas are difficult and messy. There are many versions of truth. But, one thing is clear, we've just lost another "Secret Friend."

The Sixth Sense of Animals

Our group of friends, places, rituals, and routines are still intact. Our days are filled with hikes, coffee, dancing, lectures, estate sales, movies, and visiting with friends. Other people want to join us on our adventures. I am a bit bewildered by this, until I realize that we have actually created a network of real friends.

One of our friends belongs to the Menlo Circus Club, a very fancy, country club in Atherton, California. She has invited a group of us to attend a horse show. Abbey is quite excited about going to the event. We end up filling two cars and we parade proudly across the field.

Horses are jumping over hurdles as we take our front row seats. We are close enough to hear the labored breathing of the magnificent animals as they pass close by. We hold our own breath as they thrust their bodies up in the air. As they maneuver around the obstacles, I think that the flying horses may be one of the most mesmerizing sights I have ever seen. Abbey is equally entranced.

Later we walk among the horses trotting to and from their stables. Some of the riders stop to let us admire their horses. Abbey loves being around the animals and does not show any fear. The stable dogs come running over to her.

As we walk down the paths, the horses lean out of the stalls to nuzzle Abbey. They seem to take a special interest in smelling her.

I rarely tell anyone about Abbey's medical condition and almost no one asks me. I wonder if the animals have a sixth sense.

One day, I become convinced that animals have an additional ability to sense. Abbey enjoys walking through homes that are for sale. One Saturday afternoon, I notice a sign for an open house for realtors. As I pull up in front of the house, I realize I know the owners. My friend comes walking down the path toward our car. She waves as she recognizes me. It's too late to drive away now. She invites us in.

"The open house is almost over. Come on in. I completely redid the house. I'll give you the tour." I introduce my friend, Abbey, who is delighted to meet another local person. They compare names and history, and Jan thinks she may have known Abbey's family. Jan is an artist and stunning paintings hang on every wall.

A few realtors are still milling around. "Let's go out in the backyard," Jan says.

We follow her through the French doors, onto the beautifully decorated patio. Ornately carved chairs circle the glass table, and flowers hang from delicate trellises. Ceramic pots overflow with greenery.

Jan admits modestly, "Yes, my house was featured in an architectural magazine."

I don't doubt it, it looks like there may still be a photographer lurking about. Inside and out, the house is impeccable.

The Secret Friend

Abbey and I are complimenting Jan on all the interesting details, when we hear the sound of snorting and notice three chubby blobs charging in our direction. Abbey squeals and I grab her arm to protect her.

Jan laughs, "Those are my pot-bellied pigs. They won't hurt you. They are very sweet."

"Tell that to the pigs," I think to myself. The biggest one runs straight into Abbey and tries to climb up her body.

Jan rushes over and pulls the pig off Abbey. "I've never seen her act like that before. They live inside the house with me. The realtors wanted me to put them outside during the open house."

"Are you ok?" I ask Abbey.

"Yes, but they scared me," she says.

She is still holding onto my arm, and the pigs are hovering nearby.

"Let's sit over here," Jan suggests.

We move away, but as soon as Abbey sits down the biggest pig approaches her again.

"Stop it! Go away!" Jan orders. The pig retreats, but continues to stare at Abbey. "The big one is the mother. The other two are her babies," Jan tells us.

"How long have you had pot-bellied pigs?" I ask.

"A few years now. I love having them in the house with me. They like to snuggle up next to me."

The mother pig is snorting and sniffing and creeping closer to Abbey. The babies are adding to the ruckus, although they are squealing safely behind the mother pig.

Jan shakes her head, "This is unbelievable. They have never behaved like this."

"Maybe we should leave," I suggest.

"Yeah, I think we should leave," Abbey adds.

As Abbey gets up, the mother pig rushes at her again. Now, we are squealing, the pigs are squealing, and my friend is mortified.

"I am so sorry. I don't know what's wrong with her. She has absolutely never acted like this toward anyone."

"It's okay. If you hold the pigs, we'll just let ourselves out."

Abbey and I escape unharmed, but shaken.

"I'm never going back to that house again," Abbey tells me adamantly.

"I promise you, we are never going back again."

I wonder what could have made the pigs react so vehemently toward Abbey.

"Those dogs tried to bite me," Abbey says wounded.

"They weren't dogs. They were pot-bellied pigs," I say.

"They were pigs? Why do they have pigs in the house?" she asks me.

I shake my head. "I don't know. Sometimes, I think I don't know anything anymore."

When Dead Musicians Come Back to Dance

John sends me a text message informing me that he will be going out to dinner and will be home late. "Can you take Abbey out to dinner and a movie?"

I return the text. "Yes, are you going to call her?"

"Yes, I will let her know. I should be home around 10 p.m."

"We can keep busy until then."

A minute later, Abbey's cell phone rings. She panics trying to find it. Once she finally gets it in her hand, she tries to talk without opening the phone. Only a few months ago, she could answer her phone, now it has become very confusing.

She hands me the phone just as it stops ringing. I redial the number for her and put it on speaker phone. John's voice comes booming out. She is thrilled that he has called her, until he explains about the business dinner.

"Why do you have to do that?" she asks unhappily. He mentions his job and how important this dinner is for his work. She is angry.

"Just hang up the phone," she tells me. She turns away and starts to cry.

"Abbey, I don't think he wants to go, but he has to do it because it's his job."

"I don't care," she sniffs, "he should be with me."

194

The Secret Friend

"Hey, let's go have some fun. There's a new movie that just came out and we can be one of the first people to see it."

Abbey reluctantly agrees and I'm relieved. We have been together for nine hours today, and now I have another five hours to keep her happy before John gets back.

The movie is the Social Network and as we file out of the theater, I think Abbey has really enjoyed it. We are chatting with the people around us. We are all discussing what we liked about the film. Abbey says she liked it, but she has seen it before.

One of the women turns to Abbey and says, "That's not possible. This is a new film, it was just released today."

Abbey does not hesitate, "No, I saw it years ago."

Every now and then the little glitches become apparent, but we don't let facts get in the way of our beliefs.

We arrive home after ten o'clock, but I do not see John's car. I walk Abbey to the door which is always left unlocked now. The apartment is dark and I realize we are home before John. We turn the lights on, unpack Abbey's stuff, and plug in her cell phone.

"Maybe John went to bed," Abbey says as she walks down the hall to look for him. I look at the clock, it is almost ten thirty.

"Abbey, let's call John and find out where he is."

John answers right away. "Hi. I'm still in San Francisco. Abbey, you should just go to bed. I'll be home in a little while."

Abbey is not pleased. "When are you coming home?"

"We are getting dessert and then it's going to take me an hour to drive home. Abbey, just go climb into bed."

"No, I'm not tired."

"Susan, you must be tired, you should just go home."

I'm exhausted, but there's no way I would leave Abbey alone.

"No, I'm not tired either. Abbey and I can just hang out together until you get here."

Now, this is when the secret friend scenario gets tricky. I cannot leave Abbey, but I don't want to look like a babysitter either.

"Hey, since we're not tired, let's listen to some music on your new iPad."

John has just given Abbey an iPad for her birthday.

"What's that?" Abbey wants to know.

"It's awesome that you have an iPad. I'll show you how to get it to play music." The iPad is sitting on the dining room table and we sit down in front of the magical device.

I search for the songs Abbey loves to hear. Suddenly, Wilson Pickett is playing "Mustang Sally" and we start singing along with him. Abbey is swaying and tapping her feet.

"Do you want to dance?" I ask her.

"Yeah, let's dance." I pump up the volume and we start dancing around the dining room. Next, I find a concert where

196

great artists keep coming out and jamming together. Ray Charles, Little Richard, and a parade of other music greats, jump from one classic tune to the next. Abbey and I are singing and swaying to the music.

"Wait, where's my camera?" Abbey wants to know.

"Right here on the table," I hope she's not going to take my picture at this time of night.

"I want to take some pictures so I can show John that we went to a concert," she says, as she starts snapping photos of the iPad.

After the role of film is finished, we continue to dance and Abbey is ecstatic.

"Why didn't John show this to me?" she asks bewildered. "This is so great. I love this music."

"I do too." Slowly I begin to realize that Abbey thinks either the musicians are here or we are attending a concert with dead musicians. Either way, in this moment, I brush away these unnecessary thoughts.

She's grinning as she says, "This is the best concert I have ever been to." I realize how totally overrated reality really is.

When John stumbles in the door at midnight, we are still dancing crazily around the room.

"Look what Susan did. We went to a concert tonight."

He gives me a questioning look and I can't help myself, "It was the best concert I've ever been to."

"Really?" he moves over to look at the iPad.

"Yes, but, I have to go home now. Thank you, Abbey. Call me if you want to do something tomorrow. Good night."

Miracles, Magic, and Serendipity

I've planned a day long trip for us. We will visit a grand, old mansion with spectacular grounds and an amazing garden. It's located in a town with cute boutiques, art galleries, and an apricot farm with chickens. I research as much about the area as I can, but the experience is always unpredictable. We never know who we will meet or where the adventure will lead us.

On this day, Abbey buys a bright, orange ribbon hat with a broad brim that reminds her of a hat that her father used to wear. The owner of the art gallery has paintings of horses and Abbey remembers that her step sisters used to ride. Abbey describes her chickens to the owner of the apricot farm, and we get delicious samples and treats to take home.

We have already had a successful day as we head up the mountain to find Villa Montalvo. The grounds are massive and I park the car so we can get out and explore. Behind the mansion we discover the outdoor amphitheater and the sun-lit stage. The grounds are empty, and we seem to be all alone.

As I am wondering if we are safe walking by ourselves, I notice an older man and young woman coming down the path from the woods. Perhaps it's just the western style hat, cowboy boots, and blue jeans, but the man looks just like Bob Dylan. They stop to talk with us, and the man is electric with nervous energy. He introduces himself and his daughter. His name is Dr.

Joseph. He is just visiting the area; he is a medical doctor and needed to get away for a while.

As soon as Abbey hears that he is a physician, she blurts out that she has Alzheimer's and that she hates her doctor.

"I'm not surprised. I'm burned out. I may never practice medicine again."

"Well, I'm mad because my husband won't let me drive anymore," says Abbey.

"You should be mad because you are losing your memories," he says. I wonder if she will explode, but she is suddenly calm.

She tells him, "The medicine doesn't work."

"Find a doctor who will help you," Doctor Joseph tells her.

"Will you help me?" she asks him.

"I can cure you of Alzheimer's, but you would have to do a lot of things differently and it would be expensive."

Abbey is listening intently, "Will you help me?"

"I can refer you to doctors, but I can't help you right now. I'm too burned out."

Abbey is persistent, "Why?"

"My job is to help people, but for every person who is healed, there is someone who didn't want that person to get better."

Abbey is excited, "I would do anything to get better." I wonder if this is a miracle, running into this person, at this time.

The Secret Friend

The doctor asks his daughter for a pen and paper and writes down his email address. As he hands it to Abbey, he says, "Contact me, and I will give you the names of doctors who can help you. You need someone to help you. Do everything they tell you to do."

"My husband John will help me."

"You need to have all those metal fillings taken out of your mouth."

"Ok." I've never seen Abbey more agreeable. She takes the paper and thanks the doctor profusely. We pull out our disposable cameras to document this auspicious occasion. We take pictures of Dr. Joseph and his daughter, with and without Abbey.

Then, Dr. Joseph gives us his camera and we take another round of photos. We say our goodbyes and promise to keep in touch. As we continue our walk around the grounds, I see the doctor striding alone back and forth across the lawns. His daughter has gone to sit with her grandmother, the doctor's mother, and they watch him walking. I think about what he said, and wonder what has happened to bring him to this place.

Abbey cannot wait to tell John about this doctor. She wants to call him on the phone immediately. "I have a new doctor. He can cure Alzheimer's." Her voice is upbeat and joyful. "I want you to call him right away," she tells John.

John doesn't understand what she is talking about, "Tell me when I get home from work."

Abbey is not bothered by John's reaction. "I have a new doctor who can help me."

What a difference hope can make. When we get home, Abbey is bubbling with excitement as she tells John about our meeting. John looks at me skeptically.

I shrug, but I tell him, "One of my family members was cured by alternative medicine after the traditional doctors all gave up." I'm hoping he will seriously consider this option.

"Ok, I will send him an email."

Secretly, I am as excited as Abbey. How wonderful would it be if she really could find someone to help her?

I believe in miracles, serendipity, and magic.

Breaking Down

The next day we drop the film off at a one hour photo developing center in our local shop. Abbey is excited to show John the pictures of her new doctor. When we return to pick up the photos, the girl behind the counter tells us that there was a problem.

"Do we need to come back later and pick them up?" I ask.

"No, your film was in the machine when it broke down, so the pictures didn't come out."

"What do you mean? Are you saying that we're not going to get our pictures at all?"

The girl looks at me, "Yes." When I don't move, she adds, "But, you don't have to pay for them or anything."

I must look stunned because Abbey says, "That's ok."

"No. It's not ok," I say.

I don't want to upset Abbey, but I am outraged that the store has ruined our pictures. They are not just pictures; they are memories, important memories for someone who cannot remember. They are also pictures of Dr. Joseph and of hope. If Dr. Joseph has just vanished from the photos, does that mean the hope has disappeared as well?

"We're waiting for someone to come and fix the machine," the girl continues.

"So, there's a chance we can get the pictures," I say wanting to believe.

"Oh, no. Your pictures were definitely overexposed."

Abbey is starting to fidget, "Let's just go."

I want to jump over the counter and give her a lecture about destroying memories and hope for someone who is dying, but I'm just glaring at the girl instead.

Finally, she says, "I guess you can go take a free camera if you want."

I take a deep breath, trying to accept that the photos of Dr. Joseph are gone.

"Ok, Abbey, I think we should each get a free camera." And to the girl, I say, "Please tell your manager we are going to get our free cameras now."

The manager comes over and apologizes, while we are picking out our free cameras. I would like to explain the situation, but I cannot do it in front of Abbey, so I just say, "We are each going to take two free cameras."

He must sense my outrage, because he apologizes again, and says, "Go ahead, that's fine."

A few days go by and Abbey is still talking about her new doctor. I send John an email, "Were you able to get in touch with Dr. Joseph?"

His email is short, "I've been very busy. I haven't had the opportunity. But, I don't want to give Abbey false hope."

The Secret Friend

I consider this statement. What is the difference between hope and false hope when it comes to healing? We don't understand how spontaneous healing works, or placebos, or self-fulfilling prophecy.

How can we say what will fix her mind? Isn't false hope better than no hope at all? What would life be without any kind of hope? Isn't all hope a kind of false hope until it comes true?

CHAPTER 10 SEPTEMBER

Sacrifices, Crackheads, and Cupcakes

Fall is approaching when John tells me he wants to go to a spa for a few days. He's feeling stressed and needs some time away. I can't believe it. To me, he has been able to go to work every day, play tennis with his friends, get massages, sleep on his boat, and spend two weeks on a yacht sailing to Hawaii.

Linda says she encouraged him to go. "He has made huge sacrifices for Abbey and he needs to take care of himself." Sacrifices?

I call my sister and she is excited about returning to California. We are all set to resume our roles. I'm thrilled that Nancy is coming back. Even though she is my younger sister, she always impresses me with her knowledge, wisdom, and sense of humor.

John will be gone for five nights and compared to the marathon yacht race, this will be a simple jog. I start the planning process. We will keep the daytime activities the same, and add on a few evening outings. Nancy is the only person Abbey has allowed to sleep over, and I hope that will happen easily again.

The big day arrives. I bring Nancy over to Abbey's apartment.

"Abbey, look who surprised me." I say, "Nancy came back to visit again."

206

Abbey gives Nancy a big hug, "That's wonderful. Are you coming to Zumba with us?"

Nancy grins, "Yes, I'm going to Zumba with you, and I'm staying for a week."

"Oh good. John is going on a trip. Do you want to stay with me?"

"I would love to," she says.

I could never imagine this could be so easy. Is this another ritual? Is Abbey just comfortable having Nancy take on a caregiver role? Abbey clearly remembers that Nancy has stayed with her before. She does not seem suspicious of the obvious timing of Nancy's arrival and John's departure.

I would love to know the answers to these questions, but I do not want to risk upsetting our arrangement. Perhaps, Abbey understands on some level and is content to play her role, as well.

We have decided to drop John off at the airport again. This reinforces his departure and hopefully makes it easier for Abbey to remember that he is not coming home. John is not willing to chance Abbey's wrath, so he tells her that he is going to a business meeting.

On the way to the airport, he discusses how much he would rather stay home, but his company has made him go to this conference. He gives us an elaborate description of the work he will be doing, the other participants, and the venue. We are asking him questions about the non-existent event.

I'm thinking how convoluted this whole scenario has become and how much effort is going into the deception. Trying to keep all the stories straight is exhausting. But, it is part of the sacrifice to keep Abbey happy, so we continue to play our roles.

There's a Vessel Coming

Luckily for us, we have many fun choices to choose from to keep us active. Our friends, Dan and Coco invite us over for dinner. Six of us spend the night laughing, eating, and drinking. Abbey is participating in the conversation and even helping Coco perfect her English.

Coco's beautiful art hangs on all the walls. Abbey compliments her and tells her about her pottery. I am grateful for friends at this time. There's not a word or sign of Alzheimer's in the room. At the end of the evening, we thank our hosts and start the walk back to Abbey's apartment. We are reflecting on the lovely evening.

Everything has been completely normal, until Abbey says, "That was really nice, but, John should have been there with me." Abbey suddenly seems angry.

"But, Abbey, he had to go to that business meeting." I'm concerned that she doesn't remember. "When we dropped him off at the airport, he said he didn't want to go, but his company was making him."

"Oh, that's right." She is thinking about this.

Nancy jumps in quickly. "Abbey, we're still going to have that sleepover tonight, right?"

"Oh, yes. Now I remember." Alzheimer's may appear to disappear, but it always comes back to haunt.

My cell phone rings in the morning before I'm awake. I hear Nancy's voice whispering into the phone. "She's been up all night wandering around the house. I woke up once and she was hovering right above my face, staring at me."

"Oh, my, god, Nancy. Did you get any sleep?"

"Not really. I put her back to bed a couple of times, but she kept getting up."

"Where is she now?"

"She's on the porch. She told me that she sees a vessel coming."

"John said she could have a break with reality. Can you see her?"

"I'm watching her right now. I think she's talking to someone who's not there."

"I'll be right over." I throw on some clothes. I thought I was prepared to deal with anything, but I'm nervous about what I will have to do next. Maybe a psychological hold, or evaluation would be the best thing for her.

As I drive up in front of her apartment, I see Abbey staring into the trees.

"Good morning, Abbey! How are you?"

There is only a moment of hesitation when she sees me. "Hi. Are we going to Zumba today?"

I'm relieved. She recognizes me and she still associates me with Zumba. "Yes, we have Zumba today. What are you looking at?"

I watch her face concentrating, and perhaps sorting out her thoughts. She looks at the trees and then back to me. "I don't know. Nothing, I guess." The glitch has worked itself out, and she is back to baseline.

Our Version of Normal

We head out to breakfast. I am still watching for signs of confusion, but I don't see anything unusual. We discover an Art and Wine Festival setting up on the main street of the downtown.

Abbey wants to walk around and look for pottery. Her social skills are intact and she initiates a conversation with one of the vendors. He is a potter and a lot of his work is done in her favorite glaze. She chooses another green bowl and reaches for her credit card. The sun is shining and everything is back to our version of normal.

"I'm starving." Nancy reminds us that we have not had breakfast yet.

We choose a small, sidewalk café and sit down at one of the little tables. Abbey sits down one table away from us. We all look at each other as if trying to figure out what is wrong with this picture.

"Do you want to sit at this table?" I ask Abbey.

"Ok." She nods, but does not seem to know how to make that happen.

I look at Nancy, "Let's move over to that table."

Nancy picks up her purse and we join Abbey at her table. I wonder if the stress of John's absence is causing some of her difficulties, or if maybe it's just the lack of sleep. After we finish our meal, I suggest we go back to the apartment, so Nancy can take a little nap. Abbey agrees and we all return home. All of us fall asleep immediately. Three hours later, we wake up refreshed.

I think we are ready for the next adventure. We hop into the car and head for the sea. The Monarch butterflies winter in a grove near the ocean in a town called Santa Cruz. We walk delicately down the boardwalk searching for butterflies.

This is one of my favorite things to do. Thousands of monarchs come to this location. They will flutter among the eucalyptus trees looking for a mate. When two butterflies join together, they forget to fly. They swirl and drift deliriously through the air. I really believe that magic is all around us, we just need to look for it.

We hike around the grounds and walk the beach. We visit a few second-hand stores and eat dinner by the ocean. Nancy and Abbey sleep all the way home.

Stars, Security, and Sweet Dreams

As we are unpacking the day's treasures, Abbey wants to know what we will do next.

"Who wants to go dancing under the stars tonight?" I ask.

Abbey answers quickly, "I love dancing. I want to go."

We look at Nancy. "Could we just stay home tonight and maybe sit around the pool?" she says.

I remember that she has gotten little sleep, and I wonder how Abbey can exist on so little rest.

"You can hang out by the pool and we'll call you when we get back," I suggest.

"Yeah, we'll call you when we get back." Abbey's energy amazes me.

"No, I want to go with you," Nancy perks up and we all head out for a night of dancing.

We arrive as the band is setting up on stage in front of the town center. Every summer, Redwood City sponsors a weekly program of musical entertainment and invites everyone to dance under the stars.

I have kept this event in mind for Abbey, but until now, we have not had the chance to go. I am hoping that the crowd will be mainly families. The band will be playing music from the sixties, so I anticipate a more "mature" crowd. The musicians start to play as I am scoping out the scene.

214

Abbey wants to dance immediately. "C'mon, let's go!" she says.

"I'm not dancing" Nancy announces. "It's embarrassing."

I'm feeling a little torn now. I lead everyone over to a place near the stage. I find a place for Nancy to sit, and Abbey starts dancing in front of us. This is an ideal location. I am only a couple of feet from Abbey, Nancy is content, and the crowd looks nice and boring.

Just as I start to relax, I notice a couple of guys who look like they need an emergency intervention. They are pushing each other around in that playful, drunken stupor kind of way, and I know that it will end badly for one or both. One of them falls backward to the ground while the other one stumbles toward us. His pants are sagging, his waistband is slightly above his knees, and he can only take baby steps. I'm waiting for a spectacular face plant. Instead, he waddles in slow motion straight over to Abbey, who smiles and starts dancing around him.

"Oh, my god. Get her out of there. He's a crackhead," says Nancy. Her voice is filled with panic, while I'm trying to keep my terror under control. A security guard is standing a few feet away, and I quickly approach him.

"That guy looks like he's drunk. Can you do something about it?" I ask.

"I've already called for backup. They're on their way. I've been watching this guy and his buddy on the ground over there," he says.

I'm watching Abbey and she looks delighted that she has a dancing partner. She is even making her intense funky faces. The "crackhead" can only make tiny moves and I'm not sure he even knows Abbey is there.

The security guard and I are now about four steps away from them. I'm sizing him up. He can't weigh over ninety pounds. If he makes any threatening move, I'm sure I can knock him to the ground. Mentally, I add bodyguard and bouncer to my expanding job description.

Backup shows up, they surround the "crackhead," and walk him away from the crowd. Abbey looks disappointed to have lost her dancing partner. Then she continues dancing, accepting the loss. I am happy that she can lose herself in the moment, oblivious, and carefree.

My job is to absorb the negativity around her, protect her, and allow her to enjoy herself and life, while she still can. Abbey is smiling. The stars are coming out and the crowd is singing along with the band. It's a warm, beautiful, summer evening. It all feels perfect. I wonder what, if anything, she will remember about this night.

216

Musical Memories and Social Milieus

The next morning Nancy calls me from Abbey's guest room. Abbey is in the bathroom.

"Good morning," she says.

"Hi. Did you and Abbey get any sleep last night?" I ask.

"Yes, we had a good night. Do we have plans for today?"

"We always have plans," I say laughing.

"You do too much," Nancy tells me. "The caregivers I know don't do anything like this. They would never drive for an hour to go somewhere."

"Well, I'm not a caregiver. I'm a secret friend," I say bristling at the suggestion of being a caregiver.

"We should just try sitting on the balcony at the clubhouse today. I think Abbey would like that."

"You can try it, but I plan activities, because I think Abbey always wants to be active."

"Alright, let's try it and see what happens."

A short time later I get another phone call from Nancy, "Abbey and I were sitting on the balcony, sipping our tea, and talking with the other residents. Everything was fine and then she got up and said she had to leave. When I asked her where she was going, she said she was going home. When I asked her why, she said this was not her social milieu. What does that mean?"

I can picture this scenario so clearly and I smile. "That means she's not happy. Are you following her?"

"Yes, she's walking along the creek."

"Just ask her if she wants to take a walk. Or come over here, I found a couple of interesting things to do today."

I have found the perfect activity for us. Our local theater is hosting a "Sound of Music Singalong." The words to the songs will be provided, like subtitles.

We take our seats in the theater with the strangers around us. The lyrics are streaming across the screen.

My sister says, "Don't sing. We have terrible voices."

Who knows? Who cares? Who will remember? Abbey is singing. I'm not sure that Abbey can read anymore, but, she remembers the words to the songs. It is an interesting phenomenon, and I have seen it before with Abbey.

Music is magic. Music can still find the words in the memory banks and bring them out. Sitting in the dark, singing out loud, with a group, it is impossible not to feel wonderful. I raise my voice with the others. It's so freeing to lose the shackles of self-consciousness.

Invitation to the Alzheimer's Ball

John returns and we pick him up from the airport. Again, we talk about his "conference" and his business and how hard he worked. He says he is exhausted from his week. We tell him how much fun we have had.

Abbey is wearing her new dress from the art festival. She is bubbling with energy and glad to have her husband home. Nancy and I are counting the minutes until we can fall asleep. John wants to take us all out to dinner. Abbey does not look pleased. I realize that she wants her husband all to herself. That's fine with me. I'm too tired to eat. I suggest we go out another night.

Through emails, I tell John about our week, describing the good times and the challenging moments.

He writes, "Her doctor said that breaks with reality and visual hallucinations are all part of Alzheimer's and we should expect them as the next part of the disease."

It's hard for me to accept that Abbey is getting worse. I write back, "I can give you three examples of difficult moments, but I can also give you three examples when Abbey was brilliant and amazing."

Sometimes, I feel that John only focuses on Abbey's decline, which causes me to highlight the positives.

"We were invited to attend a fundraiser for Alzheimer's next weekend. Are you interested in going?" I ask John in an email.

I actually found the flyer on the bulletin board at the Senior Center, but I take that as an invitation from the universe.

"I think you might meet some interesting people, and even find some helpful resources."

"Maybe, can you send me the information? I don't know how Abbey will respond to going."

"It's in the town of Los Altos where her father lived, and she always wants to look at houses in that area. There will be lots of food and wine and she enjoys talking with people. I think she would like it."

I read that the guests of honor will be a couple about John and Abbey's age, who are facing a similar situation. The wife has been diagnosed with Early-Onset Alzheimer's and they will give a talk at the fundraiser.

I hope that John and Abbey will find hope and inspiration in this couple's brave battle.

John eventually writes back, "Ok, I'll get tickets for the four of us."

220

A Season of Hope and A Time for Tears

It's not until the morning of the event that I start to worry about how Abbey will react. Then I realize we will be surrounded by other people with Alzheimer's, researchers, and professionals. If something goes wrong, I hope everyone will understand and be helpful.

John drives over to pick us up. Abbey is in the front seat wearing her "Pretty Woman" dress. She looks lovely, although as Nancy later mentions, "If I had known he was going to put that on her, I would have ironed it."

John appears to have put some effort into making himself and Abbey look presentable. I have tried to impress upon him that the fundraiser is being held on the grounds of an estate and we should dress for the occasion.

The venue is impressive, with expansive lawns, tastings by notable wineries, food by upscale restaurants and caterers, live music, and a photographer. Upon arrival, we are greeted by friendly faces and each of us is handed a wine glass that says Alzheimer's on it.

Abbey looks suspicious. "Wait. What is this?"

John answers her quickly, "This is the event that I told you about. It's to raise money for Alzheimer's."

Abbey looks angry, "And why am I here?"

I try to calm her down. "Our friends from the Senior Center invited us to come here. The food is free and they have some lovely artwork that I think you might like."

Abbey looks at me sternly, "Is that all?"

"Yes, we are just here to have fun. Would you like to get some wine?"

She smiles at me, "Ok, then." With a sigh of relief we walk up to the first vendor and hold out our glasses.

We stroll along, talking to the baristas, learning about the different wineries. Abbey notices the paintings and asks one of the artists about her work.

"Oh, I didn't paint these. The artwork was done by people with Alzheimer's. I teach a class and this is some of their work."

Abbey backs up. "Oh. That one is nice. I like the colors."

The woman launches into a discussion about what people are capable of despite their disease.

Abbey listens to her nodding, "I think you're right."

I think the woman would be surprised to learn that she is talking to someone with Alzheimer's.

The food looks delectable, and we find a table overlooking the gorgeous landscaping in the back of the house. We decide to take turns filling our plates at the different stations. Abbey cannot balance a plate, but to John's credit, he walks with her, filling up multiple plates for both. He guides her tenderly around from booth to booth. Without the tension and anxiety, they move together in an equal partnership.

Under the warm, sunny skies, in her pretty polka dot dress, Abbey looks relaxed, present, and happy to have her husband at her side. The photographer snaps pictures of them side by side. All my fears disappear. They are just another couple enjoying themselves and the moment. I'm still hopeful that a miracle will occur.

After we finish eating, we wander through the maze of items being auctioned. There are impressive options, from a basket of gourmet items to a week-long stay at a condo in Hawaii.

I watch John hovering over one item. He writes his bid down on the paper. Another man is waiting next to him, and as soon as John moves away, he adds his name and another hundred dollars to the bidding list. John looks disgruntled and walks over to us.

"What did you bid on?" I ask him curiously.

"I want that condo on Kauai, so I can take Abbey to Hawaii," he says.

"I want to go to Hawaii," Abbey perks up.

"Hey, we could block anyone else from bidding on the trip, if you really want to win the auction," Nancy suggests.

"That's ok, I'm going to wait until just before the auction ends and place the last bid."

A voice announces the final two minutes to place bids on the items. John takes his place by the bidding sheet for the condo. His rival is standing nearby.

"I want John to win the auction," Abbey says, "He's never been to Hawaii, but I have. I could show him around."

John takes his time signing the sheet. His rival moves toward him. I wonder if the garden party will turn into a wrestling match. John straightens up, still holding the paper, and says something to the rival. The other man looks over at us and then back at John. He nods and concedes the condo.

I know that John has played the Alzheimer's card and won. I remember Abbey telling me that sometimes people give you things because you have Alzheimer's. She's just won the trip to Hawaii. If anyone deserves a trip to paradise, she does.

"We're going to Hawaii!" John tells Abbey.

"Yay! I'll take you to all the fun places," Abbey says enthusiastically.

John is triumphant. "Let's go claim our prize." He takes Abbey by the hand, and they look as though they could walk off happily into the sunset. The photographer is busy taking pictures. Nancy and I call him over and ask him to take some of John and Abbey. He follows them up the hill, snapping photos of them clinging joyfully together.

Another voice comes over the speaker, inviting us all to the main entrance. A podium has been set up and the hostess thanks everyone for their attendance and support. She introduces the

224

guests of honor, the husband and wife who are speaking about Early-Onset Alzheimer's. The crowd becomes quiet. The husband speaks of how devastated they were to learn of his wife's diagnosis.

"The first thing we did after we found out that she had Alzheimer's was to go directly to see a therapist. We wanted to know what to expect and how we could help each other. We know it won't be easy, but we are committed to fighting this disease together."

By the time he has finished speaking, most people are wiping away tears. Then, he introduces his wife. "She is the real hero," he says, "Because of her memory challenges, she wants to read her speech."

I'm impressed that she is standing before the crowd and reading to us. She is convinced that researchers will find a cure. She hopes that doctors will find something in time to help her. But, she and her husband have researched the likely course of the disease. They have made the difficult decisions if the worst happens. They have also decided to speak out and help other people who have been diagnosed with Alzheimer's.

She and her husband have started a support group for couples dealing with the Early-Onset Alzheimer's Disease. They are not sure what will happen next, but they will deal with the end together.

When her speech ends, she starts to cry, her husband is crying, and most of us in the crowd are crying. The hostess steps up to the podium and everyone is clapping for this brave couple. I look over at John, and see him sniffling and wiping his face. Abbey is looking at John as the tears are running down her cheeks.

"Thank you for sharing your story. Thank you all for coming. With your support, we will find a cure for Alzheimer's. Please come and meet our guests of honor," the hostess says.

"Would you like to talk with them?" I ask John.

"Yes, I'd like to know more about the support group," he says, pulling himself together.

Abbey is strangely quiet. We wait in line to meet the couple. John introduces us and asks the husband about the support group. Abbey stares at the wife. Nancy and I tell her we think she is very brave for giving that talk.

"I have Alzheimer's, too. But I'm ok." Abbey finally says to the wife.

They look at each other intently. I wonder if they are comparing themselves to each other. The silence seems awkward, but I wait, wanting to give them time to think and say something to each other.

Finally, the wife says, "It's a nice day today."

And Abbey answers, "Yes, it is."

People are leaving, but we decide to go back to the cupcake table one last time. As we walk down the path under the trellis, John takes Abbey's hand again. Confronting the reality of the disease has been emotionally challenging, but it seems to have made John and Abbey closer again. We look over the sea of cupcakes still left.

"Are these free?" Abbey wants to know.

"Yes, take as many as you want," says a voice behind the table.

It's been a wonderful event. We don't want to leave. So, we fill our plates with chocolate cupcakes, topped with chocolate frosting, and chocolate sprinkles, get another glass a wine, and delay our return to the other reality for a little longer.

That night, Nancy gets a phone call from her husband. Her birthday is two days away and he wants her to come home. He has booked a flight for her the next day. He says he misses her.

I remember the way the husband and newly diagnosed wife bravely clung to each other as they described their ordeal at the Alzheimer's event. How lucky she is to have someone so dedicated to her. I remember John and Abbey, and the way they held hands at the fundraiser. All these couples have been married for more than twenty-five years. I wonder if there's a secret to choosing a mate who sticks around.

CHAPTER 11 OCTOBER

From Bondage to Barn Cats

After Nancy leaves, Abbey and I return to our routine. Of all our activities, Zumba is still the clear winner. Visiting our friend, Ray, and going to estate sales with Coco are our next favorite things. We are back to feeding the birds at the duck pond and hiking up hills. The gem shows are still fun, and we attend any musical event that is not too expensive, or far away.

Still, change is in the air. I ask Abbey if she wants to go to a pumpkin patch. Experiencing the changing seasons will keep her in touch with reality. She remembers going to the farms when she was a child and is eager to go again.

As we drive over the mountain, the fields are orange with pumpkins. Many years ago, I made this trip with my children. As I pull up in front of the farm, we see a small train chugging around the property.

The ponies are carrying excited children in a circle. Abbey can't wait to get out of the car. She wants to pet the goats and the ponies. Abbey grins when they nuzzle her hand. The simplest things are gratifying now.

"Take my picture with the goats," she says, as she poses next to the goats, which are nibbling at her hair.

"OK, good. I got it," I say.

"I used to have goats," she remembers.

228

"You had two goats, didn't you? What were their names?"

"Hmm. I don't know."

"Was it something like Yassameh and Gossamey?"

"Maybe." I realize that Abbey's stories have fewer details. This was something she always used to know.

"I want to take your picture," Abbey tells me. I hand her the camera and watch her turn it over until the lens is directed toward her face. She pushes the button and snaps another photo of herself. Oddly enough, these photos are usually very interesting. The angles are unusual, catching parts of faces, bodies, flowers, and strange shadows.

When I look at the photos Abbey has taken, I think this is a tiny lens into the world as she sees it. One of her unintentional photos was taken while she was seated in the passenger seat of my car. She was leaning out the window pointing at something. She caught her own image in the side view mirror taking the picture.

Another photo captured raindrops on the windshield with a stop sign in the background. Some photographers struggle for years to capture the unique images that Abbey takes so effortlessly.

Abbey flips the camera around and points it at me. We have a little routine that must look comical to bystanders. Abbey holds the camera at arm's length, not even bothering to try to look through the lens. She points the camera in my general direction. I move around trying to get my head into the picture. She tilts the camera downward; I squat down so she will photograph my head and not my boobs.

I don't consider myself photogenic. I have always hated having my picture taken. I usually have an awkward look, or my eyes are half closed, or I'm in a strange pose. However, Abbey has taken four pictures of me and I love every one of them. I have shown them to other people and received amazing compliments. My daughter said I look twenty years younger in one of them.

Abbey plunks herself down on one of the pumpkins and makes a silly face. I wonder if she was always so confident and self-assured. She is comfortable being the center of attention and enjoys having people compliment her antics.

Country music is playing on the speakers and Abbey jumps up and starts doing a little dance. "My sister should have married that cowboy; he owned a lot of land. She would be really rich now."

Abbey has told me this story before. I've asked her sister about the cowboy, but there's no recollection of any such person. According to her sister, there was no cowboy, no Indians were stolen and forced to pan for gold, and Abbey never went sailing with her father; Linda was the one freezing on their father's sailboat.

"I really like this cowboy music," Abbey says.

"Me too," I join in the dance around the pumpkins.

We go home with two Cinderella pumpkins, three brightly colored gourds, a jar of local honey, and a new glazed pot. We carry our treasures into Abbey's apartment. I arrange them on the dining room table.

"Tell me what we did again today," Abbey asks as she looks over the booty.

"We went to the pumpkin patch and your favorite place to buy pots. Oh, and we bought some local honey from that farm stand."

As I mention each place, I point to the corresponding souvenir. Abbey nods and then says confidently,

"That's what I thought."

John walks through the door and sees all the new stuff.

He raises his eyebrows, "Did we really need another pot?"

I look at Abbey and remember how happy it made her to pick it out, and how it helps bring back the memory of the day.

I smile at Abbey, "I'm pretty sure that you did need another pot, right?"

Abbey makes a sassy face, "Uh-huh, I needed that pot."

A Certain Kind of Hell

The next morning starts with tears. I can hear the shouting before I even ring the doorbell. He answers the door in a huff. She is crying and threatening to divorce him. He wants her to wear her khakis with the leather belt. From my perspective, that outfit is a problem when she needs to use the bathroom. Sometimes she cannot unbuckle the belt. She has had a couple of "accidents" due to this problem. I have mentioned this to him, but he is still insisting that she wear it.

"Is that a new belt?" I ask innocently, "because, I'm pretty sure that I threw the old one away. Or, maybe I just wanted to."

He gives me a little smirk. I am probably overstepping my boundaries, but I am spending ten or more hours a day with Abbey. By now, I know what works for both of us.

"I don't want to wear it," Abbey says.

John looks unhappy. "We need to go to see the lawyer today," he says, "Your sister is coming to meet us. You want to look nice."

"You just want to send me away," Abbey sobs. I freeze as I look at John.

"I didn't say I was going to send you away," he says unconvincingly. He turns so I cannot see his face. "I have a meeting. I have to go in to work. Linda is going to bring you to the lawyer's office. I'll see you there."

She is still upset and refuses to answer. He concedes the clothing battle and walks out door.

"He wants to send me away. That's why I have to go to see the lawyer," she says. The little quiver in her voice gives me goose bumps. "I'm going to ask Linda to help me."

I know why they are all going to the lawyer's office, and she is not totally wrong. She is not being sent away, just yet, but plans are being arranged for what seems inevitable. To watch yourself fall and not be able to stop it, must be a painful kind of hell.

"I'm sure Linda will help you. She's your sister and she loves you very much," I say. The words are comforting to Abbey. We all want to believe that someone will rescue us in our time of need.

"I'm going to talk to Linda about this," she says.

"That's a good idea," I say, "Your sister will know what to do."

"What time is it?"

I check the clock. "Nine o'clock. Linda is going to get here around noon."

"Do we have time for coffee?"

"Sure. We have plenty of time."

"I don't want to wear these pants today."

"You don't have to. What do you want to wear?"

"I want to wear the swirly skirt."

"I love that skirt. You look so pretty in that skirt. Let's go find it." These are small details, but they give Abbey a sense that she still has some control things in her life.

After we get Abbey into her comfortable clothes, we move over to the dining room table to collect her things. I notice a huge box of Godiva Chocolates sitting in the middle of the table. After the stress of the morning, a nice piece of caramel filled chocolate would be deliciously soothing.

"Abbey, would you mind if I have a piece of chocolate?"

She looks at the box, "Of course not, help yourself."

I don't even care that I am going to eat chocolate before breakfast. With great anticipation, I remove the lid of the box. I blink a couple of times. I'm trying to make sense of what I see. There are no chocolates. The box is stuffed with what appears to be bright red chicken feathers.

"Abbey! What is this?"

She looks at the box and smiles, "Oh, that's my rooster, Ramon."

"Why is he in the box?"

"Because, he's dead." She gives me the look that indicates she cannot understand why I would need to ask a question with such an obvious answer.

We drive to our favorite Starbucks at the mall. I park in our favorite spot under the tree. Abbey leans forward and tries to get out of the car, but the seat belt pulls her back. She tries again

234

without success. I make an obvious effort to remove my seatbelt, but she is still confused. I try another strategy.

"Is that seatbelt sticking again?" I say.

"I think it is," she says, still tugging on the strap. Abbey seems to have forgotten how to remove her seatbelt.

"Do you want some help with the seatbelt?"

She sinks back into the seat, defeated. "It's bondage. Alzheimer's is a kind of bondage. I hate it," she says.

Sometimes her insight and ability to verbalize her condition shock me.

Time passes until Linda sends me a text message. "I'm almost here. Who should I call?" It's always weird to be sitting with Abbey and sending text messages about her.

I write back. "You can try to call her on her cell phone. But, I will drive back to the apartment now."

"Ok, I'll meet you at the apartment," she writes.

We pull up in front of the apartment and find Linda standing on the sidewalk. She opens her arms as she walks toward us. "Hey, kiddo, come give me a hug," she says.

Abbey is looking for the door handle. I quickly unclip her seatbelt and Linda opens the door to help her out. Abbey melts into her big sister's arms. It's a touching moment filled with promise. I know that Abbey feels that she can depend on her sister to protect her.

Later, Linda calls me in shock. "It was awful. Abbey cannot even sign her name anymore. She was embarrassed. I was embarrassed. She cried. It just broke my heart."

As soon as Linda says this, I realize that I have been watching Abbey forget how to write her name. When I met her, she could still sign her name. Over the past nine months, her signature has dissolved into a scribble.

At first, her letters started to melt into each other. Then, she wrote fewer letters. Eventually, she would draw an X, or a crooked line. One time, I'm pretty sure she wrote, "Go to hell," but there's been nothing like that for a long time. Now even her signature is flat lining.

Cages, Incarceration, and Dreams

I plan an especially ambitious trip for the following day. I hope it will erase the unpleasantness from the visit to the lawyer's office. We are driving up the mountain to Skyline Boulevard. Redwood trees are towering over us. Occasionally, from a scenic outlook, we glimpse the breathtaking sight of the bay area.

Over the deep, green tops of the forest, the land drops away to meet the shimmering, blue water. The bay is speckled with sailboats, and the bridges look like shiny crowns. We drive past the sparkling waters of the reservoir, where sea birds are swooping and diving. We have the windows down, and it is a glorious day to be surrounded by breathtaking beauty. It is a day where all things seem possible.

Knowing how much Abbey loves plants and animals, we are on our way to visit a location that promises to have both. All the trees and plants are labeled in nurseries and botanical gardens. It's like having a cheat sheet to rely on.

It has only been a few years since Abbey received her degree in botany. To accomplish this, she had to memorize hundreds of names of plants. Presumably, the names are still filed away in her brain, but the retrieval system is broken. Sometimes, the names come tumbling out and she glows with a sense of accomplishment. Sometimes the names remain elusive and her frustration grows instead.

"Have you been to the cactus garden at Stanford?" she asks me.

"I didn't even know there was a cactus garden," I say.

"I'll take you to see it. They have a lot of rare succulents."

"Succulents. I would love to learn the language of landscaping."

She is pleased now, "I can teach you."

"Okay, but you might have to remind me sometimes."

She smiles, "It's ok, sometimes I forget things too."

We are reassuring each other. I hope these moments make her happy. I hope that she can stay functional for a long time, and when the serious forgetting starts, she will also forget how much she has forgotten. Losing your mind is painful enough, but watching the pieces disappear has to be torture.

Today, we are going to the Mountain Nursery and Gardens. According to their website, the extensive gardens are spread around the property and connected by charming pathways.

One trail passes a hidden pond stocked with fish and frogs. A quaint shop offers tea and sweets inside the old barn which has been lovingly restored by the family who lives on the property. Art by local artists will be on display. Goats, chickens, and other farm animals are allowed to roam about as they please.

From the Japanese garden to the California natives, everything will be labeled. We will merge with nature, we can touch and smell anything we want, and other people with

238

landscaping knowledge can talk "plants" with us. It is out in the middle of nowhere and nature will be wild and abundant. This destination has all the ingredients of a successful adventure.

Suddenly, I notice a giant wooden play structure set up on a hill just off the road. Massive ropes are hanging between the tall poles. It looks like a huge monkey cage.

"Did you see that?" I ask her as we drive past.

"No. What was it?"

And then, I realize what we have found and I turn the car around to go back.

"I think this is where Koko lives. You know, the gorilla who learned to communicate through sign language."

"I know about that," she says. She seems less excited than me, but I am thrilled enough for both of us.

"I don't know if Koko is still here, they were building a place in Hawaii, where she could run free." I have always wanted to see Koko, and it seems fortuitous that we should have found her home today.

I park the car. "Let's walk over and see if Koko is outside today."

She seems hesitant, but I am still talking about how amazing it is that this gorilla learned to communicate, and how sweet it was that she had a little kitten she took care of. I know she loves animals, and I assume that she would love to see this gentle giant swinging from the ropes.

239

As we reach the edge of the property, she stops walking. "Wait," she says, "There's a gorilla inside that cage?"

I look at her with mild surprise. "Well, that's a play area, but I guess she lives inside. We'll be safe, she can't get out."

"I'm not going." She says adamantly. "I hate it when animals are in cages."

"Well, this is a really nice cage, and I think she has a whole house to herself." I'm thinking to myself that Koko gets to live in one of the most expensive places in America, and she probably has a bigger home than both of us.

But it's not enough for her. "I hate cages," she says, "Nothing should be in a cage." She starts to walk back to the car.

I look up the hill forlornly, and then turn to follow her.

"Do you ever go to the zoo?" I ask her.

"No. It makes me mad to see the animals locked up in cages." She seems upset.

Oops. How did I not know this?

"I don't see Koko anywhere. I think they must have set her free in Hawaii." I am trying to fix this quickly.

"Let's go find the nursery and see the plants."

I had no idea that she felt so strongly about cages. When my kids were little, they jokingly called the aquarium the fish prison. This story would not amuse her, so I keep it to myself and make a mental note to avoid talking about any kind of incarceration with her.

The trip to the nursery erases the unpleasant incident. The goats and chickens are plentiful and wandering around freely. We spot a couple of deer and red-tailed hawks. The barn cats approach us and rub against our legs.

A friendly woman tells us how it was always her dream to live on this mountain with her family. Abbey tells her that all she wants is a house, and a garden, and a little dog. The woman says that if she wants it badly enough, she will get it.

CHAPTER 12 NOVEMBER

Champions and Heroes

Darkness is coming earlier these days. Usually, around three o'clock, Abbey will want to know what time it is. She does not want to go home until she is sure John will be there. As the sun goes down, she gets more anxious.

When I bring her home, I always wait with her until John comes through the door. I try to coordinate our arrivals with John, but lately I feel like I am nagging him. In emails, I am asking him for estimated departure and arrival times. He is uncomfortable being asked to commit to specific times.

"We are spontaneous people," he says, "We don't like to plan things."

I find this frustrating, and perhaps a bit annoying. Like most people, I left spontaneity on the delivery room floor. Children need to be cared for, fed, and changed on a predictable schedule, not when the spirit moves them. This is just part of the parental skill set that comes with having children.

I realize that Abbey is his spouse, and not his child. But, the disease has stolen a lot of her adult decision-making and reasoning skills. She has in many ways regressed to the state of a child.

A bright spot occurs in the growing darkness of fall. The San Francisco Giants win the World Series and Abbey is thrilled. She insists on going to the Giants paraphernalia store. She wants to buy a shirt with the San Francisco logo.

Suddenly, everyone is a fan, and lines weave around the store, waiting to buy merchandise. Everyone is talking about how wonderful the Giants played and how long it's been since the Giants won a World Series.

Abbey tries on every hat in the store at least twice. She also wants to buy a shirt for John. The decision is excruciating for the salesperson, who is trying to help us. Repeatedly, I encourage him to help someone else who already knows what they want, but he sticks with us. He asks Abbey if she is from California.

"Yes, I'm a native," she says proudly.

"Where were you born?" he asks her.

"In Washington. In, um...what's the name of that town?" she asks me.

"Uh...is it Tacoma?" I ask her.

"Yes!" She turns back to the man. "I was born in Tacoma."

He looks confused, "I thought you said you were a native."

"I am a native," she insists.

It's time for me to jump in, "Where were you born?" I ask him.

"I was born here."

"Me too," Abbey says.

"What high school did you go to?" I continue the conversation as if nothing were amiss.

"East" He is looking back and forth at us.

I look at Abbey, "Did you go to West High School?"

"Yes, my sister went to the other school, but I went to West."

Before he can ask another awkward question, I grab a silly hat and ask Abbey what she thinks about it. Then, we go back to our challenge of finding the perfect San Francisco Giants shirts.

When John gets home, Abbey wants to give him his present right away.

He sees the bag and says, "I can guess what's in there."

Abbey opens the bag and looks inside. She looks surprised.

John says, "Show me what you've got."

Abbey pulls out two shirts and looks as though she has never seen them before.

John is grinning at Abbey. "Which one is for me?" he says.

"I don't know," she says, bewildered.

"I like this one," John says.

Abbey looks unsure, "Do you like it?"

"I do," he says. And he puts it on to show her. He puts the other shirt on her.

She is happy now as she says to John, "We can wear them when we watch the game tonight."

244

"There aren't any more games," he says. "The Giants won the series. We watched them win last night."

She pauses, but, refuses to admit that she forgot. She gives him a look, "I know that."

John doesn't challenge her. "Hey, there's a huge celebration in San Francisco tomorrow. A million people are supposed to show up. Maybe, you and Susan can go."

Abbey looks enthused, "Yes, let's go!" she says.

"Sure, call me in the morning if you want to go," I say. Even as the words come out of my mouth, my brain is thinking this is the most preposterous idea I have ever heard.

Why would he suggest such a potentially dangerous activity? In what universe could this possibly be a good idea? But now that John has planted the idea of going to the celebration, I go home and research the event.

Hordes of people are expected to swarm the city. Most people are taking public transportation into San Francisco. There will be a parade of players through the streets of the city, a ceremony to honor the players, partying, drinking, and general mayhem throughout the day, and into the night. It will be a rare event to attend, something that may not happen again, ever. Still, the thought of taking Abbey into a crowd of a million drunken, out of control strangers seems insane.

I know that John and Abbey still ride their bikes through the streets of our town. John said he was amazed Abbey was able to maneuver through the obstacles around town. They have been married for over thirty years. This may be a risk he is willing to take based on something they have discussed. But, I am not willing to risk her life.

When Irrational Exuberance Makes Sense

When I go back in the morning, Abbey is wearing her Giants shirt and John raises the issue again. "Are you going to San Francisco today for the big party? I wish I could go with you. It's going to be incredible."

"Maybe," I say "Do you want to go, Abbey?"

"I want to go. I love parties," she says.

"Good. Do you want to get coffee first?" I am stalling for time. My first priority is to keep Abbey safe. My second priority is to keep Abbey happy and entertained. My mantra is still the same, nothing bad will happen to Abbey on my watch.

Abbey struts into Starbucks and the baristas call out to her, "Hey Abbey, good morning! Love your San Francisco Giants tee shirt!"

Abbey is glowing. Everyone is talking about the crazy celebration in San Francisco.

"Susan and I are going to see the Giants today." Abbey tells everyone.

Our Starbucks friends are impressed, and we have moved up a few notches on the cool scale. "Wow! It's going to be wild! You have to come in tomorrow and tell us all about it."

"Yes, we're really excited about going," I tell them. Even as I say the words, I'm wondering how I will bridge the gap between what is real and unreal.

After we finish our coffee, I suggest we go to the clubhouse at our apartment complex to see if anyone else wants to go with us into San Francisco.

As we walk up the stairs, the clubhouse manager calls to us. "Hey, come on in. The parade is starting. It's on the big screen in the theater room."

Abbey urges me to hurry up. "C'mon, I don't want to miss this," she says.

The room is dark, except for the light from the hallway and the live feed is playing on the movie screen. I recognize another resident who is already there and we exchange greetings.

Abbey and I sit down just as the announcers are being introduced. The other resident tells us that her daughter and family are at the parade, but she didn't want to deal with the crowds.

James, our wonderful club manager, brings bowls of popcorn and glasses of lemonade to us. Abbey leans over and whispers "We got really good seats. Do you know that man?"

"Yes, I do," I say. This is the truth.

"This is really cool," she says.

I can tell how happy Abbey is feeling. I realize that she may think we are actually at the parade. I see no reason to take that away from her. For the next two hours, we have a front row seat, we're riding the trolleys with the players, watching confetti fall from the sky, listening to the crowds of people cheering, and experiencing the joy of the day.

We can see much more of the festivities than the sweaty, boozy, bodies squeezed together in the city. We have avoided the traffic jams, and saved money on gas and trains. I have kept Abbey safe and happy, and overall it has been a fantastically successful day.

When John gets home, he immediately wants to know if we went to San Francisco.

Abbey is bubbling with joy. "Yes, we went to the parade," she says, "Susan knew someone and we got the best seats."

John looks at me and raises his eyebrows, "Really?"

"We had a blast! We got to see the parade and the players. It was awesome," I say.

"We had popcorn and lemonade," Abbey adds. It amazes me that Abbey can remember what we ate, but not realize that we were sitting in the clubhouse.

Later, we will need to discuss the larger issue of confusion, but right now, Abbey is elated. She also thinks I have important connections. I'm feeling exuberant. It may be irrational exuberance, but it still feels good.

Super Heroes and Slaying Zumba Dragons

Abbey is still upbeat when she phones me the next morning. "Hi! Is it a Zumba day?" she says.

"Yes, do you want to go?" I say.

"I'm all ready to go."

"Ok, I'll pick you up."

I hear a voice in the background. Abbey giggles, "John said that's his job." We have played this skit before.

"Ok, John can pick you up, and I will drive you to Zumba." We all laugh. It's an easy start this morning.

But the pieces are starting to crumble. We walk into the Senior Center with our entourage. Our friends greet us warmly, "The Zumba ladies are here!"

"Come to Zumba with us," Abbey encourages everyone. Our little group sashays down the hall toward the sexy salsa music.

As we take off our jackets, the Zumba teacher calls me over. "Can I talk to you out in the hallway?" she says.

"Sure," I say, suspicious of what is coming. I motion to one of our friends to keep an eye on Abbey. She nods.

"You know I've always been supportive of Abbey coming to class. I just adore her. But, I want to tape our class today. Can you keep her out of the way, you know, like on the side of the room, or in the back?"

I can't believe that the teacher would suggest something so offensive. "I cannot and will not tell Abbey where she can stand in the class. You have a lot of other classes you can tape. We only come to two classes a week. Why don't you use another class?"

"I need to tape this class today. Can you just keep Abbey out of the class for about 15 minutes?"

"No. The magic for Abbey is being normal, just like everyone else. And you're asking me to tell her she can't be in your video and that she has to stand outside while you tape everyone else? Really?"

"Listen, you always told me to tell you if there was a problem with Abbey in the class. I never mentioned it, but some people feel uncomfortable having her in the class. In fact, some people don't want to come to class if she is there."

"Wait, are you telling me that you don't want Abbey in the Zumba class?"

"You told me to tell you when it became a problem."

"First of all, I drive most of the people who take this class here. They are all friends of Abbey and they wouldn't come to this class if they didn't want to. Who said they didn't want her in the class?"

"I'm not going to say. But, I have lost some clients because of Abbey."

I don't believe this for a moment. Abbey has always been treated well by the other Zumba participants. We have been taking the class for nine months now and this is the first complaint I have heard. The other dancers are always inclusive and protective of Abbey.

The only issue with Abbey's participation is that she will sometimes drift into someone else's dance space. We accept it and dance around her if that happens. The tradeoff is Abbey's passion for the class and her obvious joy from music and movement.

"Abbey has just as much right to be here as anyone else," I say, "In fact, she probably benefits from the class more than anyone else."

"That's why I didn't say anything to you. I really enjoy her energy in class."

I still don't believe that anyone has complained about Abbey, and I'm feeling pretty angry about this conversation.

"We are going to go back in there and do Zumba," I say, "I am not going to tell Abbey anything. She can dance wherever she wants. You can tape another class. We are not going to say anything about this to Abbey."

The teacher and I are both furious at each other, but we put big smiles on our faces as we return to the dance room.

"Everyone ready for Zumba?" the teacher booms out. I smile at Abbey and she smiles back. She is my friend, and no one will take this joy away from her.

The Secret Friend

That night I explain the situation to John. I want him to share in my outrage and defend his wife against this travesty. He sounds sympathetic, but strangely resigned. "That's unfortunate. But, you had a good run while it lasted," he says.

Where's the man she married, the man to carry her out of a burning building? I want him to be her hero, to go slay dragons, or at least insensitive Zumba teachers. Instead, he sounds too tired to fight.

"She's pulling everything apart in the house tonight. I asked her what she was looking for. She said, she's not looking for anything; she's just trying to remember. I better go check on her. Talk to you tomorrow."

CHAPTER 13 DECEMBER

Demons, Darkness, and Voodoo

The despair of December sets in early. Each day the theme seems to be the same. Abbey is upset with John. John is mad and jealous.

It's Sunday morning, my one day off. I am sitting in the clubhouse, enjoying brunch with friends, when I get a text message from John: "Abbey is going to call your phone. Don't answer."

My phone rings and I see Abbey's phone name appear. I decline the call. The next buzz tells me I have a phone message. When I play the message back, I can hear John and Abbey's heated conversation. She wants to go somewhere and he wants to stay home. I delete it without listening to the whole scenario. My phone rings several more times, and John is sending more text messages.

Finally, I ask a friend to walk over to their apartment with me. When we arrive, the door is open and I see John sitting alone on the sofa.

"C'mon in," he says, making no effort to get up.

"Hi. Where's Abbey?" I say.

He sighs deeply, "She got mad at me because I didn't want to go do something with her," he says, "I'm just too tired. She ran out the door."

254

"Do you know where she went?"

"No, but she'll probably find her way back, or someone will bring her back."

"When did she leave?"

"About fifteen minutes ago."

I can't believe he is still sitting there. "Aren't you worried?"

"I'll go look for her in a few minutes. We had a big fight. We just need to cool off," he says. This makes sense under normal conditions, but I am astounded at how nonchalant he sounds.

I look at the friend who accompanied me over to the apartment. She is standing there with a look of disbelief.

"Why don't we just take a look around and see if we can find her," I say.

John is annoyed with me, but he follows us out the door. As we walk down the sidewalk, I hear Abbey yelling his name. He walks toward her slowly. As soon as she sees him, she starts screaming at him. "Where were you? Why did you leave me?" My friend and I quietly slip away.

Susan Bostian

Strong Women, Snakes, and Sea Nymphs

I find an interesting exhibit at the Cantor Art Museum on the Stanford Campus. It's called Mami Wata, Arts for Water Spirits in Africa and Its Diasporas. The traveling exhibit will examine the images of Mami Wata, or Mother Water, in different cultures around the world.

At first Abbey is reluctant. "I've been to that museum a lot of times," she says.

"This is different," I say, "It's a special exhibit about strong women in Africa, Brazil, and other countries around the world."

"Oh, I like art about strong women," she says.

"Let's check it out. If we don't like it, we can leave." Other than the written descriptions from the college website, and a picture of a brightly colored painting of a woman and a snake, I don't know much about it.

As we enter the gallery, I see Abbey's face light up. A dark skinned woman in an exotic dress is standing in front of a picture of women and snakes intertwined together. Abbey's reaction tells me she is interested. I have timed our arrival to coincide with a tour.

The docent invites us to join the small eclectic group. Together we enter a strange and wondrous world where women are depicted as goddesses and devils. Life size models are dressed in authentic African garb. Some paintings depict the beauty and

256

desirability of women. Women are the nurturers and the caretakers of the world.

"But, Mami Wata is also powerful," our docent tells us, "She is different from Eve who was tricked by the snake in the Garden of Eden. Mami Wata can control the snakes."

Some pictures warn men to be aware of her powerful charms. It is the juxtaposition of good and bad, reward and punishment, divine and hell, worship and fear, birth and death, and life and destruction. It is all the misunderstandings, mistakes, and magic associated with women.

There are Barbie dolls with missing heads, paintings of sea nymphs, a music video of ritualistic dancing, and a shrine to a spirit, where visitors are encouraged to leave trinkets. It is dark, disturbing, and strangely fascinating. Abbey loves it.

At the end of the tour, the docent tells us that a Voodoo Priestess is coming to the museum and invites us all to come back and see her.

"I want to do that," Abbey whispers.

"Ok, I'll find out when she will be here and we'll come back and meet her." I realize that this sounds like a weird thing to do, but after all, Stanford is hosting her. How bizarre could it be?

No Direction Home

Abbey's difficulties are increasing. She still wants to take photos, but she is taking more of her face and feet now. Over and over, she turns the camera, trying to find the button to take the picture.

One day, we are making the journey home after spending a fun day in Mountain View. We are traveling on the El Camino Real, which means the Kings Highway. It leads directly from one town to the other. Abbey has ridden on this road for over sixty years.

Abbey asks me, "Where are we going now?"

"We are going home, unless, you want to go somewhere else," I say.

It's after five o' clock and John has said he would be home by six.

"Why are we going in this direction?" she asks me hesitantly.

"Well, we were in Mountain View today, and now we are going home to Palo Alto."

"Why are we going to Mountain View?" she sounds emotional.

"We are going home to Palo Alto. John said he was coming home early tonight."

"But, we're going in the wrong direction," she says looking all around.

258

The Secret Friend

"We're going in the right direction to get home, I promise you." I try to say this gently.

Abbey is looking out the window and there is silence in the car. Then, I hear her crying softly.

Susan Bostian

Let the Festivities Begin

Linda has invited John and Abbey to come to her home for Christmas, but she has some concerns. "We have a couple of special dinners and parties to attend. Would you help Abbey buy a couple of nice outfits to wear?" Linda asks me.

"Abbey is having a more difficult time dressing and undressing, but we will find something appropriate," I say.

After coffee the next day, Abbey and I walk around the mall. Abbey is looking forward to going to see her sister.

"Do you want to find a party dress to wear at Linda's house?" I ask her.

"Yes. I know what I want," Abbey says. I am not surprised.

She points to a shiny green blouse in a store window. It is perfect for a festive, holiday celebration. We march into the store, find the top, and bring it to the register to pay.

I greet the cashier, "Hello, my friend wants to buy this blouse."

"Do you want to try it on?" the cashier says, looking at Abbey.

I look at Abbey. "It's your size, it should fit you. Do you just want to get it?" I say.

I hope the cashier will not interfere, but she does. "It won't take long to try it on, that way you can make sure you get the right size," she says.

The Secret Friend

Abbey considers this advice. "I guess I should try it on," she says. She places the blouse on the counter and starts to remove her shirt in the middle of the store.

The cashier looks shocked, "The fitting room is over there."

Abbey looks confused. I look at the cashier with daggers.

"I think the blouse is perfect for Abbey, don't you?"

She finally understands, "Oh, yes, yes, it is."

"Ok, Abbey, you don't need to try it on. It's perfect for you," I say.

Abbey is relieved, "Oh, good. I hate trying things on."

I look back at the cashier, "So, now, we're just going to buy this blouse."

This time she does not protest.

Predictions and Pressures

Stress is building and it's more than just the seasonal pressures. I am sending more requests to John to coordinate our departure and arrival times. He reluctantly sends information, some of it is relevant, and some of it is just ridiculous.

"I don't need to know what you are doing, or where you are," I tell him, "I just need to know when I should plan to be with Abbey. Please give me estimated times of departures and arrivals."

"It's hard to predict how much work I get done in a day, or how much traffic I might hit on the way home," he says.

He sends me an electronic calendar, with a couple of scheduled meetings, and a dental appointment. I am so frustrated with our lack of ability to communicate, I am actually wondering if he is deliberately trying to piss me off.

One morning I wake up at six, shower, get dressed, gather my papers with the day's activities, and wait for the phone call. We are supposed to start early today. But by eight o'clock, there's been no communication. I send John a text message asking what time I should come over. There's no response. I'm starting to feel cranky.

Finally, around nine o' clock, I get a text message from John. "Slow start today. We woke up late. We will eat breakfast now," he says.

Really? Had I known I would have liked to sleep in, too. More time passes. Ten o' clock comes, and another text arrives.

The Secret Friend

"I'm going to take Abbey to the DMV with me. We need to register her car. I'll call you after lunch."

That feels like a deliberate attempt to annoy me.

The Stuff of Life and the Life of Stuff

The next day, Abbey calls me early in the morning and we are off on our routine. After coffee, we head out to an estate sale in a wealthy town of Hillsborough about 20 minutes away. The location is promising and we have been invited by the organizers.

The internet has made this job much easier, allowing me to stay informed about events of interest to Abbey. I am on the mailing list for gem shows, gallery openings, pottery shows, science exhibits, nature hikes, musical events, special museum happenings, health fairs, lectures at universities, community gatherings, and an odd assortment of funky, fun alerts.

Abbey and I have refined this list based on how much we have enjoyed the adventures. Sometimes, I read the description of the estate sale to Abbey, so we can predict how interesting it will be.

Abbey pointed out early on that "rich people have the best stuff." Except for the man who had a secret stash of rare sea shells from around the world in his garage, we have found this to be true. I pull up in front of a huge mansion on a hill.

"This is going to be good," Abbey announces.

Part of the allure of the estate sale is getting to do all the forbidden things that society doesn't allow. We get to march into a stranger's house, go through their rooms, closets, dresser drawers, and personal items. It is a fascinating experience to examine someone's life, without having them watching over your shoulder.

The Secret Friend

Each life is spread out and on display in front of you. Trophies, framed academic certificates, books, bras, jewelry, cheap kitsch, museum quality furniture, dead plants, original paintings, hemorrhoid cream, silver spoons, animal slippers, and wedding gowns.

We have seen an original cape made for a bullfighter in Spain. We've giggled at a lot of regrettable clothing choices. We've snickered at the collection of tea cups from every state in America. We've seen a few items that were unidentifiable. We've learned about some quaint cultural pieces such as the silver silent butler.

We've made every mounted talking and singing fish perform, and rolled our eyes at all the ridiculous golf trinkets and trophies. Every time we find one of those copper colored, fondue dishes, we say the same thing. At some time in American history, everyone must have bought one of these contraptions.

In an estate sale, everyone is invited to ogle all the stuff you have collected throughout your life, from your accomplishments, to your underwear. World travelers like to bring back mementos from exotic locales, which become tangible memories to connect them to the places they have been.

When someone dies, their treasures gather dust, or get adopted by family members. The unwanted stuff ends up in the estate sale, getting dispersed back into the world, collected by someone else for a time, until the next transition. Some things will end their existence in the dump. But, perhaps even there they will be rescued, or recycled.

At one particularly fascinating sale, all the contents of the home belonging to an attorney seemed untouched by relatives, or friends. His framed credentials hung on the wall, the file cabinets were stuffed with his papers, and his closets were filled with clothes in bags freshly returned from the dry cleaners.

The photo albums were stacked in the study. I opened one of them. Faces of anonymous people, smiling and laughing filled the pages. I wondered where they were now. I turned the page. There were pictures of an older man, perhaps seventy years old or more. The man is grinning at the photographer, as he poses knee deep in a lake. He is standing there naked, the family jewels totally exposed.

I bring the album over to our friends who have organized the sale. "These are personal pictures," I say, "I wonder if the family might want them."

The woman shakes her head, "The family said they didn't want anything. They said we should sell what we can and dump the rest." Usually, families fight over the deceased person's stuff. I wonder why no one wants his stuff.

But today's estate sale reflects joyous and loving lives. The walls of the home are covered in happy, family pictures. Children, grandchildren, even great-grandchildren cluster together in photos taken at celebrations, holiday parties, and in exotic destinations.

This couple has collected fine furniture, expensive jewelry, and hand carved curios with colorful figurines. This home is filled with an abundance of art, beauty, and family. Gorgeous kimonos hang on the walls. One whole table is covered with dragons and gargoyles.

Pictures of the happy couple are sprinkled throughout the rooms, but they are not for sale. The general mood of the buyers is upbeat and positive. People are talking to each other, and we are enjoying the whole experience.

I buy a little glass bird. "Look, Abbey, I am going to buy the blue bird of happiness," I say.

Abbey finds a small green, ceramic frog which delights her. "I'm buying this one, frogs are good luck," she says.

When we get to the car, I offer to put the little frog in the back seat, but Abbey insists on holding on to it. She keeps it cradled in her hands, occasionally stroking it. I hope the good luck will rub off on her.

Just as we are about to head home, John sends me a text message: "Got to go to a meeting tonight. Probably going to be late. I know Abbey will be angry. I will call her."

I know that she will probably explode when she hears the news. I pretend to look for something to delay starting the car. Abbey's phone rings, and as she is trying to find it, she dumps her whole purse upside down and everything falls to the floor of the car. She puts her purse up to her ear and says hello.

The phone rings again. She looks at the purse and says, "I hate this purse." I see the phone down by her feet.

"Abbey, there's your phone, let me get it for you," I say.

"Hurry up. I think John is calling me," she says.

Just as I pick it up, John hangs up. But he calls back immediately. Abbey is giddy, until she hears that he will come home late.

"What? No, It's not ok," she says, "It's just a stupid job."

John starts to explain, but Abbey just hands me the phone. "I want a new husband," she says. And she begins to cry.

"I'm sure John would rather be here with you, and not at some boring, business dinner," I say, "I've been to those kinds of business things and they're not fun." I try to comfort her and she tries to be brave.

"Do you want to go out to dinner with me?" she asks.

"I would love to," I say enthusiastically.

"Let's go to that place, you know..." she cannot remember the name, and I need to guess what she is thinking.

"Uh, Buck's?" I say.

"Yes, that's it," she says. Actually, Bucks is located next door to the Woodside Bakery, which is where we usually eat now, but we call both places Buck's.

268

Fishing for Change

Abbey and I are seated at a table for two. The waiter brings some bread and balsamic vinegar for us. We both ask for the fish and chips. Abbey orders a beer. She reaches over and takes the napkin off the table next to us, even though her napkin is sitting in front of her.

Abbey takes a bite of her bread, and then drops it in the dish of vinegar. When she cannot find her bread, she reaches over and takes the bread off my plate. By the end of the meal, all the bread, and her fish and chips are in the vinegar. She is eating directly from the balsamic vinegar dish.

We are talking and laughing as usual, but something has changed. I had wondered if I would recognize the time when we could no longer go out and blend in. I think now it will be obvious.

We get home and the apartment is still dark. I put the lights on and Abbey walks through the apartment calling out John's name.

"He had to go to that business dinner, I think, but he should be home soon," I tell her.

"Did he tell you that?" she asks me suspiciously.

"I think I heard him say that when he called you on your cell phone," I tell her tentatively.

"I want to call him," she says.

"That's a great idea. Let's find your phone," I say. I dial John's number and put the call on speaker phone. He doesn't answer.

"Where is he?" Abbey wants to know.

"I don't know, but I heard that there was some good music on television tonight. Do you want to see if we can find it?" I say.

Abbey agrees and I start flipping through the channels. I am ecstatic to find Mick Jagger singing and dancing across the screen.

Abbey is thrilled. "Let me get the camera," she says excitedly.

I pull a new camera out of the box, and Abbey takes thirty-six photos of the television screen. After the roll is exhausted, we dance and sing for over an hour with the Rolling Stones, until John finally comes home. I shut off the television.

Abbey looks very pleased. "John, you missed it. Susan and I went to the best concert tonight. The Rolling Stones were there," she says.

"Yeah, John. Abbey and I have been dancing and singing with Mick Jagger and you missed it," I say.

John is looking a tad confused.

"Thank you, Abbey, for a wonderful night," I say, "Call me if you want to do something tomorrow." And I roll myself out the door, and drop into my bed like a rock.

270

Breaking The Spell

Christmas is coming, the days are flying by, and the water in the creek is rising. Abbey is excited about going to see her sister for the holidays, although her sense of time is getting foggier.

Some days she will get nervous and tell me she needs to get home to pack. One day, she wants to buy a Christmas present for her nephew. When he was a baby, Abbey named him "The Critter." He is now about five years old.

"I want to buy a camera for The Critter so I can teach him how to take pictures," she says.

We settle on a package of disposable cameras, like the ones we use to document our adventures. But by the time we get home, Abbey has forgotten that the cameras were for someone else. John's work has become more demanding, darkness is arriving earlier, and John is coming home later.

John warns me ahead of time he will be home late one night. I search my listings to find something that Abbey will enjoy. I discover the Voodoo dance performance at the Cantor Museum. The same people who brought the Mami Wata exhibit to Stanford University are sponsoring this unique dance troupe.

The founder of the dance company is bringing her mother, who is a Voodoo Priestess. Attendees are strongly encouraged to participate. I remember that Abbey said she wanted to go. The timing is perfect.

I pick Abbey up in the morning and John tells her he will be home late. "Money. I want money," Abbey demands holding out her hand. John pulls a fifty dollar bill from his wallet.

"You should take Susan out to dinner tonight," he says.

"Then I need more money," she says.

He hands her a couple more twenty dollar bills. Keeping track of her credit card is challenging, but cash is a nightmare. I'm trying to remember how much she has and where she is stuffing it. Later, I will try to put it in the zippered pouches of her purse, in case the contents of the purse spill out again.

The day passes quickly. Abbey wants to visit Ray, and he takes us on an extensive tour. We eat lunch, take a hike, and go home to get ourselves ready for the dance.

"I'm not sure what it's all about," I tell Abbey, "But, I think it has something to do with the Mami Wata exhibit and a Voodoo Priestess is going to be there."

"Do we get to dance too?" Abbey wants to know.

"That's what it said in the invitation, but we'll just have to go and find out."

"That's ok," she says. Abbey's enthusiasm for adventure is intact.

As we enter the museum, I am wondering what kind of person would go to this performance. We are directed to a large room, with chairs arranged in a huge circle. Almost all the seats are taken, and someone is scrambling to find more chairs for the few people who are standing.

The group is mostly women, and if I had to guess, the men are the "plus ones" in this crowd. This appears to be a culturally curious, enlightened group, as opposed to some wild, fringe, spell casting crazies. But it's early in the night, anything could happen.

Abbey and I sit next to the drummers. A beautiful woman introduces herself and explains a bit about her life, her religion, the role of strong women, and the importance of water to the world.

Four women appear, dressed in long flowing blue and white gowns to signify water and purity. Each dancer is balancing a jug precariously perched on her head. Their movements suggest the dangerous journey the women must take to bring water to their families.

Despite life threatening challenges, the women continue to risk their lives. These women are the life-giving forces and the caregivers for their families. They are willing to sacrifice themselves for love. The story is painful and heartwarming; the women rely on each other and the magical deity, Simbi Dlo, the Goddess of Water, for survival.

The artistic director introduces her mother, Florencia "Fofo" Pierre. Fofo is a Mambo, which means she is a Priestess in the Voodoo religion. Mother and daughter teach us to sing a prayer to Simbi Dlo, asking for her presence, protection, and life-giving resource: water.

There are about fifty of us in the room, and we start chanting quietly. Abbey has been listening intently and now her lips begin to move, repeating the incantation to Simbi Dlo. The drummers beside us make low, rhythmic sounds. The drumming intensifies and our voices grow louder. The dancers pass by each of us, reaching out to us, and pulling us in. The Voodoo Priestess invites us to join her in performing a dance to please Simbi Dlo. No one in the room moves.

Abbey looks over at me, "Can I get up and dance now?"

I smile at her. "Absolutely, yes."

Abbey walks right up to the Mambo and starts to dance alongside her. Abbey has broken the spell, and everyone else in the room gets up to dance too. I grab my camera and try to take photos of Abbey and the Voodoo Priestess dancing together. I want Abbey to remember this moment.

A woman, who is dancing, frowns at me and says, "You should be experiencing this, instead of trying to take pictures of it." Under different circumstances, I might snap back. But I'm not annoyed. This is a lesson. We know so little about the people around us, and what each of us is going through.

I look at Abbey dancing in the light, in the middle of the life force, participating, surrounded by acceptance and love. She too has walked a hard road and the most difficult part of her journey lies ahead. But, in this moment, she has come far, and she is glowing. I imagine that others around her may be fighting their own battles.

274

The Secret Friend

We need more ceremonies like this, to come together, to share strength and love. Even for me, there needs to be a time for healing, for getting back up, and joining the dance. I think of the moment before Abbey got up to dance, when everyone else in the room hesitated.

Abbey was the inspiration for everyone to come together. When Abbey asked me if it was okay for her to get up, she knew she could trust me. We have become the best of friends. We have learned from each other. I know it's time for me to rejoin the dance. At the end of the evening, the Voodoo Priestess thanks Abbey for being the first one to get up and dance. I take a picture of them with their arms around each other.

The halo of joy follows us home.

A Season of Stress

The next morning, I show up at their apartment. John is unhappy.

"He's just mad about the money and jealous about how much fun we have," Abbey tells me.

"What did you do with the money?" John wants to know. He looks at me. "Abbey put her purse somewhere and now we can't find it," he says.

I've seen this scenario before. The purse will be found under a pillow, or in the dirty laundry, or somewhere no one would expect it to be. Usually, John has a more Zen-like attitude about these disappearances, but he seems especially tense today.

Abbey is mad. "Why are you talking about me?" she says, "I'm right here."

John realizes his slip-up. "I'm not talking about you," he says, "I'm just telling Susan what we're doing."

"Well, I don't like it!" she says, anger apparent in her voice.

"Sorry. I'm just stressed," he says, "I need some prescriptions picked up before we go to visit your sister."

"That's your job," she says, "And the medicines don't work anyway."

"I'm going to work now" he says. John has given up.

"I want a new husband!" she says, as he walks out the door.

The Secret Friend

We flap our arms to shake off the stress, we drink our coffee, and we even walk around the shoreline and feed the ducks. The dark cloud of the morning is still lingering.

I send John a text message: "Abbey is still upset. Will you call her?"

It takes a while, but he eventually gets back to me: "I'll call her," he writes, "Will you pick up the prescriptions and bring something home for dinner?"

"I will try to work it into our day," I respond.

He writes back: "Thanks. Also, the bookstore has the book I ordered. Will you pick it up? I'll pay you back."

I feel like sending him a text: "I am the secret friend, not the secret servant." But I restrain myself. Everyone is stressed out these days.

We go to visit our friend, Ray, but he is not around today.

When I pull into a parking lot, Abbey wants to know where we are going. Luckily, the drug store is next to the Goodwill Store. Abbey is delighted to find out we are going shopping. Everyone will get something they want today.

She picks out a dress and a vase and looks happier than she has all day. We walk into drug store and get in a long line to pick up the prescriptions. This is how you know the holidays are here, I think to myself, everyone is rushing out to pick up their drugs to deal with all the "holiday happiness."

We are talking about Abbey's new dress and inching closer to the pharmacist. Finally, it is our turn, and I lean over the counter and say softly that I am picking up the drugs. I'm worried about Abbey overhearing me, so I'm making hand motions to keep it quiet.

Suddenly, Abbey calls out, "John! John!" and takes off after a man in the store.

"I'll be right back," I tell the pharmacist, "Can you have the drugs ready?" I'm chasing after Abbey, who is running after some stranger.

He doesn't look much like John. Once he turns around, Abbey quickly realizes that she does not know him. "Oh, sorry," she says.

"He really did look like your husband from the back," I say empathetically.

I steer us back to the pharmacy, scoop up the drugs, and we walk back to the car. "Would you like to go to Kepler's and look around the bookstore?" I say.

"Sure. I like to look at the books," she says.

I open her car door and cringe as I watch all the contents of her purse fall to the ground. It's dark now and I can only hope that we have all of the items. We make it to Kepler's and I leave Abbey looking at a table of books, while I run over to the information counter to pick up John's book. He has ordered a book about Alzheimer's and I ask the woman to hide it in a bag immediately.

278

"I have to pick up some groceries. Do you want to come with me?" I ask Abbey.

"Is John home yet?" she says.

"Hmm. I don't think so," I say, "Do you want to call him?"

"No. I'll go shopping with you."

While we're walking through the store, I ask Abbey, "Do you want to get any groceries?"

"No, that's John's job."

I decide we will make this easy. I buy two cooked chickens and a couple of side dishes that are already prepared. At the checkout, I tell the clerk to put the items in separate bags.

John sends me another text message, "Got a call from the police department. Someone turned in Abbey's wallet," he writes.

I text back, "she dropped her purse in the parking lot of Walgreen's. I thought we had picked up all items."

"I could pick it up," John offers.

I reply, "Good, I've already picked up the book, drugs, and dinner. We are heading home."

We carry Abbey's stuff into the apartment. "I have to go to the bathroom," she announces.

"Ok, I'll be here," I say.

As soon as she closes the bathroom door, I sprint out to the car and grab the bag of groceries. I want to slip them into the kitchen before she notices. Maintaining this performance is becoming more exhausting.

I can hear water running, but I'm not concerned, until I hear Abbey scream. I run to the bathroom and shove open the door. I can see her cringing in the corner of the glass shower, steam rising around her from the burning hot water pouring from the showerhead.

Frantically, I run across the room to her. As I am sprinting toward her, I step in a warm pile of poop on the floor and see the feces rise up between my toes. I keep running and shut the water off, so she will not be scalded.

"Are you ok?" I ask her.

"I had an accident," she says crying.

"It's alright. It happens to all of us," I tell her.

"Let me see you. Did you get burned?"

"No. I'm ok," she says. She must have gotten out of the way, because I can't see any burns on her skin.

"I'm going to put the water back on so we can wash you off," I say. I am calm on the outside, but I'm shaking on the inside. I wash her off and stick my foot in the shower to rinse off the poop.

By the time John gets home, we are both cleaned up, and only the soiled towels remain. I go home and use the Lysol wipes to clean between my toes. Then I collapse into my bed. I wonder how much longer I can keep this up.

The Secret Friend

When the Magic Well Runs Dry

I frame three photographs from the Alzheimer's event and give them to John and Abbey as Christmas presents. It is the only thing I do for Christmas. There is no tree. No presents. No Christmas dinner.

My daughter is spending the holidays with our family back on the East Coast. She calls me on Christmas morning. I hear the joyful voices of family members chastising me for not participating in the festivities. I'm happy for them. For me, I am not in the mood to celebrate. All I want to do is sleep.

At some point, I make my way to Starbucks. I am filled with gratitude when I see the sign that says, "Open Christmas Day." There are quite a few people at Starbucks today. The baristas are cheerful, they already know what I want to drink, and I am grateful for this small bit of joy. Then I return home and go back to sleep. I need a break.

But, there are no breaks in the Alzheimer's world. As soon as John and Abbey return from Christmas with Linda, John sends me an email. He has decided to take some vacation days. He wants to spend time on his boat, go sailing, play tennis, and take some time to relax. Abbey is eager to see me again. I am the maker of magic, but I cannot conjure up enough energy to jump back into my role.

I send an email to John, "I'm really sorry, but I need a few days, too. If you need some help, I know someone who said she is available."

The Secret Friend

John sends me an email, "Abbey does not want to go out with anyone else. She only wants you."

I am almost too tired to feel guilty, "I'm sorry, John. I just can't do it right now."

I realize this means no income for me, no vacation for John, and no magic for Abbey. But, I honestly cannot jump back into the performance. The well of magic has run dry.

CHAPTER 14 JANUARY

When the Winter Winds Come

A couple of days later, John sends me an urgent email. He has reached his limit with Abbey. He needs to write an important email, and he wants me to take Abbey out now.

The general barking tone of his message pisses me off, and begins a flurry of email discussions. In my email response, I finally tell him how frustrating and disheartening it is to be treated without respect or appreciation:

"I have worked extraordinarily hard to create a world of friends and activities for Abbey, and I have kept her engaged and happy for the past year."

John's response is equally harsh, "I think this is over," he writes, "Abbey needs more structure. You have been extraordinarily reliable and resilient. It was too much for you to maintain by yourself. I will start to look for alternatives."

His response simply escalates my frustration. I write back, "I have been available every time I made a commitment, except for the time I was in the hospital. I have found replacements for the few times when I was not available. You have sabotaged all of my suggestions for helpers, and undermined many of the activities I created with Abbey."

John sends me an email response.

"Your email was over the top and I did not like it in general. I think we are all kind of burned out and pissed off at each other right now. I hope my email response was diplomatic enough that you are not surprised to get this email from me.

"However, your actions helped motivate me today to challenge Abbey. From the time I woke up, I said it was time to stop pretending that she was okay, that she has a very serious illness, and she needs more structure in her life.

"I told her I was paying you a lot of money to come take her out every day, and that enabled you to do it, but it was not sustainable, that five days a week was too much, and furthermore, you might not be available anymore.

"She shrugged and did not seem to care (about me paying you), she just said you were a friend, and of course that was all that mattered.

"But, I was making the point that it was too much for me, you, and Linda, and something had to change starting today. I said I wanted her to go to an adult day care program."

I am in shock. With one vindictive, devastating blow, our whole magical world has come crashing down. To take away a year's worth of joy, from someone who is terminally ill, seems to be the cruelest act imaginable.

As I try to imagine how she must feel, I am overwhelmed with sadness. My heart is broken and I cannot stop crying. I would never have gotten involved in this situation if I had thought it might end this way. My intention was always to bring happiness to

Abbey, never heartache. With all these emotions bubbling inside, I sit down to write an email back to John:

John, I am very disappointed that you have repeatedly ignored my requests for communication regarding departure and arrival times. You have been inconsiderate of my time by keeping me waiting and then deciding to take the day off or run some errands or go to the DMV or promising to be home and then not showing up until much later.

My goal was to make Abbey happy. To do this I had to get to know her, learn her likes and dislikes, history, family and friends. I also incorporated what we know about brain stimulation, exercise, socialization, healthy habits and good nutrition. When we started, Abbey was wandering around alone, unable to find her way home, losing her purse, her cell phone, her credit card, not even able to remember to eat during your absence. She was depressed and lonely.

Through exploration and adventures, we built a world of friends and activities she enjoyed and loved. We have traveled from Crissy Field and the museums of San Francisco, to the botanical gardens and thrift shops of Berkeley, hiking Alum Rock in San Jose, exploring Villa Montalvo's gardens, browsing shops in Los Gatos, visiting farms in Saratoga, searching for pumpkins in Half Moon Bay, chasing butterflies in Santa Cruz, attending pottery shows at Foothill College, gem shows in various locations, lectures at Stanford, dances in Redwood City and Cantor Museum, mingling with animals and in gardens at Hidden Villa, hiking trails at Shoreline in Mountain View, photographing deer at

286

Foothill Park, and birds at the shorelines, tracking down treasures at estate sales, seeking out obscure nurseries up on Skyline Boulevard, singing along with the Sound of Music production and many times in the car, joyously participating in the Holi Festival dancing with hundreds of people covered with colors, and numerous other adventures in a multitude of towns up and down the peninsula.

We have made friends with other residents of our complex, dancing buddies at numerous Zumba locations, found a network of people at the Senior Center, and many others who we have encountered during our outings, including Ray.

When Abbey wanted to see her stepmother, I located her and drove Abbey down to visit. I brought Abbey to the newspaper offices to see her former coworkers. I have kept in touch with Sally, her other friend, encouraging her to join us at Zumba, and bringing Abbey to her house for tea.

I brought Abbey to a Sunday service at the church her father built so she could meet the people who were enjoying the place her father had created. I introduced Abbey to the people who run the school her father built. We organized a luncheon with friends at the Arts Guild. We have documented our trips with brochures and photos.

In addition to the hours I spent during the day with Abbey, I spent many (unpaid) hours every night researching activities and planning days that would keep her engaged and make her happy.

I am Abbey's friend. To state the obvious, she has a devastating, terminal disease. She must be terrified as the fog of confusion takes over her mind. I thought we all agreed, as Linda so succinctly put it, that we would make her last cognitive months happy. As you once said, the magic is that she is normal when she is out with me. I have done everything I could think of to create that magic and keep Abbey happy every day.

My heart broke when I read you told her I was being paid to be her friend. I cannot think of any act that would be crueler and more hurtful to her. I can only imagine that you have reached a point where you can no longer maintain the status quo. Maybe the sleep deprivation, anxiety, stress, and sense of loss have become overwhelming for you. This may be the time to re-evaluate the total situation with a professional or someone with more expertise in this area."

John's email response.

"Susan, I have complete respect for you and what you did for Abbey over the past year. I still see you will have a place in her life as a friend. She values your friendship. I want to enable this.

"If it seems like I am firing you, this is not true. In addition, I was not being mean by telling Abbey I have been paying you over the past year. In fact, she accepted it immediately. It is all part of being reality-based, while she is still somewhat rational; she needs to know that I am doing things to help her. I do think it is time for you to get a real job, but I would like you to continue on a part-time basis, with some conditions to be determined."

The Secret Friend

Over the next week, we try to untangle our miscommunications and rebuild a relationship that will work for all of us. Unfortunately, the damage appears to be beyond repair.

With each email, John's words torpedo the efforts. "You have not communicated effectively or used your time appropriately. You have not spoken to me ONCE. You just went into hostile bitch mode, I do not respond well to passive/aggressive women. We are going to have to do some work on this. You have had a greatly positive influence on Abbey over the past year. We have lots of common "grounds." But we are both new at this, and we have made mistakes along the way. I am the one writing the checks, so my decision is final."

We exchange a few more emails, but I cannot find a way to establish an acceptably sound foundation. I am very emotional whenever I talk about Abbey. The visits to the day care centers are unsuccessful. All the other possibilities fail to work out.

John sends me another email. "Abbey wants things to go back to normal. She wants a friend again. Normal means you come back. Five days a week works for me. Abbey misses her "friends" which you enabled."

I feel so guilty. I miss Abbey, too. But each time I try to imagine a scenario to rebuild a life for Abbey, John's words come back to haunt. I realize that in our society, caregivers are underpaid and underappreciated. I remember when I insisted on being called a secret friend, not a caregiver. But, even John, who should have understood what taking care of another person entailed, was demeaning in his comment when he said, "It's time for you to get a real job."

I have learned a valuable lesson from the Voodoo Priestess. The Mami Wata ceremony recognized sacrifice and celebrated the caregivers as valued members of society. They know that society depends on caregivers, just as caregivers depend on society. It takes a village to raise a child. It takes a compassionate village to care for the young, the old, and everyone between. Everyone in the village should be a caregiver.

I am a caregiver. I take care of others. I like taking care of others. I'm good at it.

What I am not good at, is taking care of myself. I'm not good at valuing myself. I'm not good at offering myself a drink of water or a break when I need it. Maybe I need to appreciate myself. Maybe I need to put energy into me. Maybe a good place to start is to walk away from people who call me a hostile bitch.

Suddenly, I realize how much I have learned from Abbey.

I tell John I cannot find a way to resurrect our world. John has burned the bridges, the town, the forest, and all the materials to rebuild anything.

John sends me an unexpected email, "Don't worry about it. I am working on finding another caregiver. In the meantime, I want to explore if you and I can become better friends. Perhaps we could play tennis sometime, secretly."

I think back over everything that has happened in the past year. I consider this odd proposal, from someone I once considered an ideal mate. I hear Abbey's voice when she told me to find someone who would carry me out of a burning building.

I think she is in an inferno, and he is leaving the building without her. I know personally how badly the burns from betrayal feel. John can never be anything but Abbey's husband. I don't care how many pieces are missing, Abbey is my friend. I would never betray the bonds of our friendship.

For the next couple of months, I see John and Abbey walk by my apartment. Sometimes, they ring my doorbell, or call my cell phone. Mutual friends tell me that Abbey is looking for me and asking if anyone knows where I am.

She does not look happy when I see her go by, but I cannot help her now. I can barely help myself. I wonder about what we created, and if it was the right thing to do.

Abbey's sister offers some comfort; in an email, she writes: "When I saw Abbey with you, I was amazed. I had not seen her that happy since she was a child. You made her last cognitive months enjoyable. This was the happiest year of her life."

Shortly after that, I get an email from John. He and Abbey will be going to Kauai. This is the trip he won at the Alzheimer's fundraiser. He says that Abbey is excited about going to Hawaii.

They are bringing a couple of family members. I hope it will be a special trip for all of them. I had worried that John would not bring Abbey on this trip. I know that it will require extra effort, but I still feel she deserves to go. It feels like the right ending for our journey.

Later, John sends another email. The trip was meaningful for both, but it was time for another change. He is moving to a penthouse overlooking a marina. He asks if I will meet with him, before he moves. When I walk into their apartment, I am shocked to see all traces of Abbey are gone.

"Where are all Abbey's things?" I ask.

"I moved Abbey to a residential care facility. She has some clothes, but she really didn't need much. I gave the rest of her stuff to Goodwill."

Her stuff is gone. Her beautiful pots, her little green frog, her connection to self and to the world. He's thrown away all the breadcrumbs; she will never find her way back home.

I ask him where the nursing home is located. He tells me no one is supposed to visit her for a month, and I need to be put on a list of authorized people to see her. He says that after he returns from a trip, he will contact me and let me know when I can visit her.

He encourages me to visit him in his new penthouse by the yacht club. He mentions the name of the nursing home inadvertently. I go home and start searching the internet to find Abbey. I discover the facility and call to verify that she is there.

I'm nervous about going to see her. It's been six months. I wonder if she will remember me. I put my pink scrunchie on my wrist. She might be angry. I try to prepare myself for that possibility.

The Secret Friend

I drive up a long, winding road and turn the corner. The bright pink villa is perched on the top of the mountain. It is surrounded by a tall black iron fence with a locked gate. I remember Abbey's reaction to Koko's enclosure. There is little difference between the gorilla's home and the dementia facility. Abbey was right, there are many kinds of cages. Sometimes, our worst fears may be premonitions.

Someone buzzes me through the locked gate. The woman at the front desk asks me to sign in, and then I am escorted downstairs through two sets of locked doors. The attendant and I stand there scanning the room, looking for her among the sleeping bodies slumped over in wheelchairs.

Then, I see her standing across the room. At first, she looks at me uncertainly, and then a huge smile breaks out on her face.

She walks toward me, "You!" She throws her arms around me, hugging me so tightly I can hardly breathe. I start to think she will never let me go. Eventually, she stands back to look at me.

"Hi Abbey, it's me, Susan."

She makes one of her obvious faces. "I know that. How did you find me?"

"John told me that you were here."

"Does John know that I'm here?"

"Yes, I believe he picked this place for you."

She seems briefly disappointed to hear this and then says, "How are you?"

"Good. Abbey, do you want to sit down and talk?" She looks much thinner, but also much the same as I remember. We talk about all the fun we had and the silly things we did together.

I finally have the courage to ask her, "We're still good friends, aren't we Abbey?"

"Of course. You're my favorite," she says.

I am greatly relieved. "You're my favorite too, Abbey. And you're my hero," I say. We sit there smiling for a moment. "Abbey, you know what I'm going to do? I'm going to write a book about our adventures and tell everyone how brave and amazing you are."

"I know I am," she says. This makes us both laugh.

"Really, Abbey, I want people to know how much you taught me," I say.

"I had to teach you a lot," she says, as she rolls her eyes.

"I want everyone to know about all the wild and crazy things we did."

"Don't forget about Zumba," she says.

"Abbey! I brought Zumba music with me. Do you want to dance?"

"Of course, I do!"

I ask the attendant if we can play our Zumba music. She takes my disk and pops it into the CD player. Shakira's voice comes out loud and strong. "There's a werewolf inside, she wants to come out. Ow wooo!"

I take her hand to guide her, and Abbey springs up. We dance and sing "Ow Wooo" around the locked ward. Some of the sleeping heads perk up and open their eyes. One of the men starts smiling and tapping his foot.

"Oooh, can I dance with you?" one of the ladies asks.

"Yes. It's called Zumba," Abbey says.

Abbey reaches out to take the woman's hand. "Here, I'll show you how to do it."

And there, in a locked ward, I saw the magic. Despite her challenges, Abbey was still one of the bravest, most compassionate people I had ever met. Abbey was not afraid to get up and dance and she made everyone around her want to be more alive and fearless, including me.

"Abbey, we will always be the Zumba ladies. I will never forget that. I'm going to tell everyone you were never afraid to get up and live."

And that's what I have tried to do.

Abbey, my dear friend, I hope I have kept my promise to you.

The End

CHAPTER 15

What I didn't say to Abbey

I'm sorry. I had hoped we would find the miracle or the magic to beat Alzheimer's disease. I am still hopeful that a cure will be found. Alzheimer's sucks. Alzheimer's is a dreadful, heartbreaking, mind stealing, life destroying monster. It is a black hole that sucks everything around it down into a void with no chance of escape. Someday, someone will break the code. I hope it is sooner rather than later.

Why Would I Tell Everyone What We Did?

I learned a lot from our experiences. I'm willing to share our story hoping someone else might benefit from what we did right and from our mistakes. Researchers say that the rise in neurological disorders will reach epidemic proportions in the coming years. Sharing our story might add to the increasing awareness of this problem. I hope awareness will lead to more support for research, and ultimately, a cure.

Some People Will Want to Know What's Real

I have come to realize that there are as many versions of truth as there are perspectives. This is my version of our history. I wrote my story based on the daily emails I wrote to John describing the places we visited and Abbey's reaction. I also printed out all the emails I had with John and Linda. I have photographs (with signage) and various pieces of "stuff" that I collected from our adventures. The blue bird of happiness will always be a special treasure. I still have notebooks with the daily schedules of activities.

We visited all the places mentioned. We attended all the stated events and activities. I had pink hair for a week after the Holi Festival. I have changed the names of some people and a few places to maintain their privacy. Otherwise, the story is accurate and honest.

I still wear my pink scrunchie to Zumba class and I think about Abbey whenever I dance.

I never imagined I would write a book about Alzheimer's, just as I never imagined that I would be someone's Secret Friend. John and I talked about writing this story together. We quickly realized that each of us had a unique perspective on what had taken place. We agreed not to discuss any details, so our memories would not be clouded by each other's perceptions. John said that he has detailed notes, and I hope that he will write his story as well.

How Time and Distance Change Perspective

Taking care of someone with Alzheimer's is like trying to learn to swim while you're drowning in the middle of a lake.

I now think Linda was right to encourage John to take care of himself. Caregivers need a break. Without help or self-care, caregivers break down and then there is no help for anyone. We were all "burned out" when everything fell apart at the end.

Instead of John and I being mad at each other, we should have been furious at the disease. But Alzheimer's is insidious. It distracts, it creates hideous dilemmas, it pits individuals against one another, and it eats away at the person suffering with the disease and their circle of family, friends, and society.

What Would I Say to John?

I'm sorry I was not more understanding and compassionate during the year that I cared for your wife. I agree with Linda; your sacrifice was enormous. Watching your wife disappear must have been excruciating. You were losing not only the love of your life but also the life you loved with her. I didn't understand the level of grief you were experiencing. I'm so happy that you got to sail, play tennis, and take time for yourself. You were a kind, compassionate, and loving husband to Abbey.

Would I Recommend the "Secret Friend" Concept to Other People?

Absolutely, yes; with conditions. Benevolent deception is a compassionate path for someone with Alzheimer's disease when their world is dissolving around them. Setting boundaries and spending limits might have extended our journey or eased the pain at the end.

Do I Have Any Advice to Give?

When falling into the abyss, ask for help. Exercise is good. Music and movement are magical.

What Did I Learn?

Abbey said all she wanted was a house, a garden, and a little dog. She was really asking for shelter, food, and love. Isn't that what we all want? When I visited Abbey in the nursing home, I told her she had gotten her big house and beautiful garden. She looked at me and said, "You know what else I want?"

I said, "Yes, a dog."

She gave me a look that almost broke my heart and said, "Just a little one."

What's Next?

Most of us have a few broken or missing pieces. We have all lost something. Life is hard and we have to be brave. But life is also fantastic, and we have to remember to feel the joy and celebrate! Abbey was always the first to get up and dance! I hope her life will be a source of inspiration for everyone.

I still believe in magic, music, and miracles.

Thank you, Abbey, for teaching me so much about living and loving.

ABOUT THE AUTHOR

Susan Bostian earned her degree in psychology at Rhode Island College, worked as Associate Editor at the Rhode Island Herald, and as a writer for the Providence Journal.

Her marriage to a Brown University professor took her to California where she continued to take classes at Stanford University.

After her two children were born, she worked at their school and created a lunch program to provide free meals for children experiencing poverty.

While living in Palo Alto, California, she met a man who proposed an unorthodox arrangement to care for his wife, who was suffering from Early-Onset Alzheimer's Disease.

As a "Secret Friend," Susan Bostian combined everything she knew about psychology, physical, mental, and emotional health, social engagement, joy and hope, and music and magic.

The Secret Friend fulfills Susan's promise to share their wild adventures as they try to live life to the fullest and outrun a savage disease. This is an honest retelling of the frustration, the heartbreak, and even the humor that is Alzheimer's.

Susan Bostian wrote "*The Secret Friend*" as a love letter to her friend and caregivers everywhere. Hopefully, this story will provide support, suggestions, and sustenance for anyone facing life's inevitable challenges.

The Secret Friend

She also writes for Medium on a wide range of subjects, including her near-death experiences, her divorce, and the shocking lessons learned in Silicon Valley.

A Special Thanks

I am forever grateful to Joe Broadmeadow, of JEBWizard Publishing, who provided the magic to bring this book back to life. Joe contributed his time, his editorial expertise, and the secret sauce to resurrect The Secret Friend.

In a strange twist of fate, Joe Broadmeadow and I grew up on the same street in Cumberland, Rhode Island. He became a Police Captain fighting organized crime. Eventually, he wrote about his adventures and created his own publishing house.

Words cannot express how much I appreciate Joe's service to our community, his courage to battle evil, and his kindness to me. Joe Broadmeadow's professional genius and generosity prove that good guys still exist.

Thank you, Joe. I couldn't have done this without you.

Susan Bostian 2025

JEBWizard Publishing
Books with Character

302

www.ingramcontent.com/pod-product-compliance
Lightning Source LLC
Chambersburg PA
CBHW071711120626
46550CB00001B/181